CAMBRIDGE LIBRARY COLLECTION

Books of enduring scholarly value

Spiritualism and Esoteric Knowledge

Magic, superstition, the occult sciences and esoteric knowledge appear regularly in the history of ideas alongside more established academic disciplines such as philosophy, natural history and theology. Particularly fascinating are periods of rapid scientific advances such as the Renaissance or the nineteenth century which also see a burgeoning of interest in the paranormal among the educated elite. This series provides primary texts and secondary sources for social historians and cultural anthropologists working in these areas, and all who wish for a wider understanding of the diverse intellectual and spiritual movements that formed a backdrop to the academic and political achievements of their day. It ranges from works on Babylonian and Jewish magic in the ancient world, through studies of sixteenth-century topics such as Cornelius Agrippa and the rapid spread of Rosicrucianism, to nineteenth-century publications by Sir Walter Scott and Sir Arthur Conan Doyle. Subjects include astrology, mesmerism, spiritualism, theosophy, clairvoyance, and ghost-seeing, as described both by their adherents and by sceptics.

The Inanity and Mischief of Vulgar Superstitions

After the execution of the Samuels family – known as the Witches of Warboys – on charges of witchcraft in 1593, Sir Henry Cromwell (grandfather of Oliver Cromwell) used their confiscated property to fund an annual sermon against witchcraft to be given in Huntingdon (Cambridgeshire) by a divinity scholar from Queens' College, Cambridge. Although beliefs about witchery had changed by the eighteenth century, the tradition persisted. Martin J. Naylor (*c.* 1762–1843), a Fellow of Queens' College and the holder of incumbencies in Yorkshire, gave four of the sermons, on 25 March each year from 1792 to 1795. Although he called the subject 'antiquated', he hoped his 'feeble effort, levelled against the gloomy gothic mansion of superstition, may not be entirely without a beneficial effect'. This collection of the four sermons was published in 1795, and appended with an account of the original events in Warboys.

Cambridge University Press has long been a pioneer in the reissuing of out-of-print titles from its own backlist, producing digital reprints of books that are still sought after by scholars and students but could not be reprinted economically using traditional technology. The Cambridge Library Collection extends this activity to a wider range of books which are still of importance to researchers and professionals, either for the source material they contain, or as landmarks in the history of their academic discipline.

Drawing from the world-renowned collections in the Cambridge University Library and other partner libraries, and guided by the advice of experts in each subject area, Cambridge University Press is using state-of-the-art scanning machines in its own Printing House to capture the content of each book selected for inclusion. The files are processed to give a consistently clear, crisp image, and the books finished to the high quality standard for which the Press is recognised around the world. The latest print-on-demand technology ensures that the books will remain available indefinitely, and that orders for single or multiple copies can quickly be supplied.

The Cambridge Library Collection brings back to life books of enduring scholarly value (including out-of-copyright works originally issued by other publishers) across a wide range of disciplines in the humanities and social sciences and in science and technology.

The Inanity and Mischief of Vulgar Superstitions

Four Sermons, Preached at
All-Saint's Church, Huntington
in the years 1792–95

MARTIN JOSEPH NAYLOR

CAMBRIDGE
UNIVERSITY PRESS

CAMBRIDGE UNIVERSITY PRESS

Cambridge, New York, Melbourne, Madrid, Cape Town,
Singapore, São Paolo, Delhi, Mexico City

Published in the United States of America by Cambridge University Press, New York

www.cambridge.org
Information on this title: www.cambridge.org/9781108044240

© in this compilation Cambridge University Press 2012

This edition first published 1795
This digitally printed version 2012

ISBN 978-1-108-04424-0 Paperback

The Inantity and Mischief of Vulgar Superstitions.

FOUR SERMONS,

PREACHED AT

ALL-SAINT'S CHURCH, HUNTINGDON,

On the 25th Day of March, in the Years 1792, 1793, 1794, 1795.

BY M. J. NAYLOR, M. A.

FELLOW OF QUEEN'S COLLEGE, CAMBRIDGE, AND LECTURER
AT THE PARISH CHURCH OF WAKEFIELD, YORKSHIRE.

TO WHICH IS ADDED, SOME ACCOUNT OF THE

WITCHES OF WARBOYS.

*Superstitio fusa per gentes, oppressit omnium fere animos,
atque hominum imbecillitatem occupavit—Multum et nobis met-
ipsis et nostris profuturi videbamur, si eam funditus sustulissemus.*
CIC. DE DIVIN. L 2. c. 72.

Cambridge :

PRINTED BY B. FLOWER, FOR J. DEIGHTON, & W. H. LUNN;

SOLD IN LONDON, BY RIVINGTONS, ST. PAUL'S CHURCH-
YARD; CONDER, BUCKLERSBURY; CLARKE, NEW BOND-
STREET, AND AT NO. 325, OPPOSITE GRAY'S-INN, HOL-
BORN; AND E. GREENWOOD, LEEDS.

M DCC XC V.

TO THE

MAYOR, CORPORATION,

AND

INHABITANTS

OF THE

TOWN OF *HUNTINGDON,*

THESE

SERMONS

ARE RESPECTFULLY DEDICATED

BY THEIR HUMBLE SERVANT,

M. J. NAYLOR.

PREFACE.

CUSTOM appears to have laid a fort of embargo upon every publication, however fmall and infignificant, unlefs ufhered into the world by fomething in form of a preface. How then fhall fermons, and thofe too upon the antiquated fubject of Witchcraft, prefume to obtrude themfelves upon the public without fuch a precurfor and apologift, to tell the caufe of their appearance, and deprecate the frowns of auftere criticifm? Of fuch a bold infringement of laudable cuftom, I will not

venture

venture to be guilty. Yet, upon the hackneyed plea of the earneſt ſolicitation of friends I will not reſt, however juſtly ſuch a plea might be advanced, but rather acknowledge myſelf actuated by a faint hope, that even this feeble effort, levelled againſt the gloomy gothic manſion of ſuperſtition, may not be entirely without a beneficial effect. Surely the ſmall mite of the poor in knowledge, caſt into the treaſury of truth, is entitled to ſome regard, eſpecially as it may excite the extenſively wiſe and learned to contribute more freely from their ample ſtores. And ſhould the following ſheets be fortunate enough to call up one combatant againſt the odious and miſchievous powers of bigotry and ignorance, my inſignificant labors

bors will be sufficiently recom-
penfed.

I am aware that by many, Witchcraft, the principal object of the
fubfequent difcuffions, will be def-
pifed and ridiculed as exploded legendary nonfenfe, unworthy even
of being ranked with thofe *pretty*
ftories which divert the nurfery, and
amufe the infant mind. Perhaps a
more extenfive acquaintance with
the prejudices and fuperftitions of
the lower orders of the community,
might induce them to look upon it
as not entirely undeferving of fome
ferious regard. Does it not fhock
humanity to fee the poor, helplefs,
infirm and old, perfecuted with ran-
corous hatred, for a fancied affocia-
tion with the infernal powers? Such
fufferers

fufferers claim our protection and fupport; fuch deftructive, uncharitable notions call for every effort to correct and eradicate them. Many, who have moved only in a fuperior fphere, and whofe minds have been cultivated by a more refined education, muft undoubtedly deem it almoft impoffible for rational beings to believe and defend fuch abfurdities. Yet ftrange as it may appear to thofe, lamentable experience but too clearly proves, how extremely deep thefe notions are ftill engraven upon the minds of thoufands, notwithftanding the great advances in learning and knowledge, which have been made within the two laft centuries. The belief of thefe extravagancies was indeed gradually yielding to the powerful progrefs of

fcience,

fcience, but of late it has again been nourifhed and revivified, in no inconfiderable degree, by the many extraordinary relations, which the late venerable Mr. WESLFY inferted in his Arminian Magazine. Numbers, accuftomed to afcribe to this great man an almoft Papal infallibility, dared not to reject what he ad anced with fuch an air of earneftnefs, or to queftion the truth of what he appeared to fanction by his authority. Their conviction has infenfibly fpread itfelf amongft the multitudes connected with them by the common intercourfe of fociety, and once more reillumined the fading flame of vulgar fuperftition. Juftice however to his fucceffors in compiling this widely circulated work, obliges me to commend them for having

b   wifely

wifely deviated from the example of their highly-efteemed predeceffor, and forborn to difgrace their Magazine, by the infertion of fuch abominable trafh.

But I fhall forbear to trefpafs further upon the reader's patience, and waving general apologies, proceed to mention the peculiar circumftances which gave rife to the following Sermons. After the conviction and execution of the three unfortunate *Samuels*, for the diabolical crime of witchcraft,* their goods, which amounted in value to 40l. were forfeited to Sir *Henry Cromwell*, as lord of the manor of *Warboys*. Averfe to taking poffeffion of

---

* For a further account of their *devilifh* deeds fee the fubjoined narrative.

the

the property of *fuch* felons, he gave all to the corporation of *Hunting-don*, on condition, that they fhould give 40s. every year to a Doctor or Bachelor in Divinity, of Queen's College, *Cambridge*, to preach a Sermon at All-Saint's church in *Huntingdon*, on the annunciation of the bleffed Virgin, againft the fin of witchcraft, and to teach the people how they fhould difcover and fruftrate the machinations of witches and dealers with evil fpirits.

The reverend and learned author of the Memoirs of the protectoral houfe of Cromwell, having mentioned this curious and ancient inftitution, adds the following uncandid reflection : *   " It is with real con-

---

* Vol. I. p. 25, fecond edition.

     " cern

" cern that I acquaint the reader,
" that there is ftill an annual Ser-
" mon preached againft witchcraft in
" *Huntingdon,* by a divine fent from
" Queen's College, Cambridge. It
" would be highly commendable in
" the Corporation of Huntingdon,
" and Queen's College in Cambridge,
" to agree, that if a Sermon muft
" be preached, the fubject of it
" fhould, inftead of being levelled
" againft the pretended fin of witch-
" craft, be an addrefs to the people,
" cautioning them againft falling
" into fuch errors and prejudices, as
" made their forefathers involve the
" unhappy and immeafurably injur-
" ed Samuels in ruin and deftruc-
" tion." Had this laborious gentle-
man profecuted his inquiries on this
fubject, with that diligence and ac-
curacy,

curacy, which is the indifpenfable duty of a rigid narrator of facts, he would have found, that the Society of Queen's were not fuch flaves of fuperftition as he ungeneroufly infinuates. The fin of witchcraft has long ceafed to be the theme of their annual difcourfes, nor has the fubject ever been mentioned, except to explode, and deprecate the lamentable effects of, fuch miferable delufions.

How far the following "addreffes to the people" cf Huntingdon are entitled to the approbation of the above-mentioned author, or how far they merit the regard of the public, is not for me to determine. Had I formed the leaft defign of profecuting the fubject fo extenfively, or of

prefenting

presenting my imperfect labors to the public, when first delegated by the Society of Queen's to deliver this annual Lecture, it would have been almoſt unpardonable not to have arranged the whole more methodically, and to have avoided the apparent repetitions which have neceſſarily ariſen from the want of a previous plan. For theſe, and other imperfections, I hope, the indulgent reader will make every allowance, which candour and good nature can ſuggeſt. I dare not be ſo preſumptuous as to lay claim to any originalities. To Dr. WATERLAND, Mr. FARMER, Mr. SHUCKFORD, and various other learned authors, I muſt acknowledge my obligation for almoſt every material obſervation theſe pages contain. If I have ſucceeded

in

in making a compilation which deserves not the severe lash of the angry critic, I am satisfied. And as my hearers were kind enough to express their approbation of these Sermons, when delivered from the pulpit, to their countenance and protection, I now again beg leave to recommend them, when issuing from the press.

SERMON

SERMON I

I Sam. xxviii. 8.

And he faid, I pray thee Divine unto me by the familiar Spirit, and bring me him up whom I fhall name unto thee.

WHETHER fuperftition or infide-lity is the greater enemy to true religion and human happinefs, has been a fubject of difpute with the Philofopher and the Divine. That both are pregnant with moft pernicious effects, has always been readily acknowledged by the humane and candid obferver. A ferious and ftrenuous endeavour to eradicate either

A   from

from the minds of men muſt therefore be
a taſk worthy of every one, who has engaged in the important office of inſtruct-.
ing his brethren. When we add hereto a
recollection of that memorable and melan-
choly event, which has given origin to
my addreſſing you this day, ſurely no apo-
logy will be thought neceſſary for pre-
ſenting you with a few obſervations upon
the curious portion of ſacred hiſtory, from
which the Text is taken. For myſterious
and unimportant as this relation may at
firſt view appear, neverthelefs, if candidly
examined, it is capable of affording us
much uſeful and appoſite inſtruction.

Saul, after having been raiſed by God
to the Throne of Iſrael, had refuſed to
obey his voice, and faithfully to execute
his commands. Provoked by this diſobe-
dience, the Lord withdrew his favor and
protection from him; and now in the decline of life, when ſurrounded by his enemies, and diſtruſting his own ſubjects, he
found himſelf abandoned by his God,
whom *he* had before preſumptuouſly for-
ſaken.

faken. Roufed by his prefent fears, rather than actuated by any real penitence for his former mifconduct, he wifhed to obtain fome inftruction and direction from above, in an exigency fo urgent and alarming. By all the various methods he could devife, did he attempt to procure an anfwer; but "neither by Dreams, nor by Urim, nor by Prophets,"* would Jehovah vouchfafe to impart the leaft comfort or inftruction. Finding himfelf thus rejected and abandoned, Saul, diftracted by the violence of his diftrefs, was determined to take a ftep at once impious and abfurd. Afflicted indeed but not humbled, forrowful yet blind to his own wickednefs, and deaf to the voice of reafon, he was weak enough to indulge a ftrange hope, that the Ghoft of the dead Prophet Samuel might be prevailed upon to liften to him, though God had deferted him. Hurried on by defpair and fuperftitious credulity, he haftily repaired to a woman of Endor, famous for her fkill in Divination and Necromancy, by whofe affiftance

* Verfe 6.

he

he madly expected to call Samuel from the dead.*

Various opinions have been advanced by Commentators respecting this transaction, you will therefore readily pardon an attempt, to illustrate and establish that, which appears to me the most rational and just.

---

* Then Saul said unto his servants " seek me a woman that " hath *a familiar spirit*,&c." 1 Sam.xxviii. the word OB, which as well as its plural OBOTH, is always rendered by our Translators *familiar Spirit*, literally signifies *a Bottle*, (which amongst the Ancients was formed of Leather, and somewhat resembled a Bladder) and was metaphorically applied to those Persons, whose Bellies, when they delivered their Oracles, were distended, like a Bottle. The LXX generally translate these words εγγαςριμυθες, *Ventriloquists*; and Isaiah xix. 3. τες εκ της γης φωνεντας *those that speak from the Earth.* This extraordinary art, or rather perhaps gift of Nature, as experience has discovered, requires not the interference of any evil Spirit. But to speak without moving the Lips, in a voice which seemed to proceed from the Belly, or from some distant quarter, might easily impose upon the ignorant and superstitious, and make them readily believe, that these responses were really uttered by *that Spirit of Divination or Apollo* (πνευμα πυθωνος Acts XVI, 16, 18,) to which they were ascribed by designing Pretenders. Such an impostor we may conclude the woman to be, whom Saul consulted.

Some

Some have thought, that the whole was nothing but a mere trick, by which the artful woman impofed upon Saul's credulity, making him believe that fhe really faw Samuel, when nothing appeared, and contriving a voice to proceed from fome fecret corner, and hold with him the converfation related by the facred hiftorian. But this opinion wears fuch an air of improbability as renders our affent to it rather difficult. For though there can be no reafon to doubt but that the *good* woman's intentions when fhe undertook the bufinefs, were to impofe upon Saul by a feigned anfwer; yet had all been left folely to her management, it is highly probable that fhe would have delivered her Oracle in terms more agreeable to Saul's wifhes. This was the general practice of Oracle-mongers, which fhe would have been induced to imitate, both by the fear of offending the King, and endangering her own life, and alfo by the defire of procuring a more ample reward. But the whole Tenor of Samuel's fpeech is much too ungrateful and folemn, much too true

and

and prophetic to have entirely originated in her invention. How was fhe able (had fhe been bold enough) decifively to declare to him, that the army of Ifrael fhould be delivered into the hands of the Philiftines, and that he and his fons fhould fall in the field? To know, and to be able, to predict with certainty, events yet fhut up in the womb of time, is claimed by God as his exclufive privilege. He challenges the fictitious Gods of the idolatrous nations, to give this clear proof of their Divinity; "Produce your caufe, faith the " Lord; bring forth your ftrong reafons, " faith the King of Jacob; let them bring " them forth, and fhew us what fhall hap- " pen; let them fhew the former things " what they be, that we may confider " them, and know the latter end of them; " or declare us things for to come; fhew " the things that are to come hereafter, " that *we may know that ye are Gods.*"* But is it not highly abfurd to imagine, that the Deity would communicate any portion of this knowledge to a deteftable

* Ifaiah xli. 21, 22, 23.

forcerefs,

forcerefs, would give her the honour of revealing his counfels, and concur with her in a vile impofition upon the credulous Saul.*

As there appears, therefore no foundation for the opinion, that all was a mere contrivance of the artful woman, to impofe upon the fenfes of her royal confulter; muft we not conclude, that there certainly was an apparition, which converfed with Saul?

But the reafons already advanced againft its being only a cunningly contrived impofture, muft equally ferve to convice us, that it could not be any familiar or evil fpirit, conjured up by the infernal power of her forceries, to perfonate the dead prophet. For this agent, as well as his

* Should any one however be ftill inclined, with Dr. Chandler, (Life of David, B. 2. Ch. 16) and other learned men, to confider the whole trafaction as nothing but an artifice of the cunning Pythonefs, yet he muft readily agree with me in the principal conclufion I wifh to eftablifh, that this Hiftory gives no fanction whatever to the popular notions concerning the powers of witches.

precious

precious miftrefs, muft have been difpofed to give an anfwer more agreeable to the inclinations and wifhes of the diftreffed king ; and both of them muft have been equally ignorant of futurity. Prefcience, it has been already obferved, is the attribute of God alone, and cannot be poffeffed by any one, but to whom, and in what degree, he is pleafed to impart it. And can we fuppofe, that he would ever be fo bountiful to beings continually engaged in labouring to counteract the defigns of his providence ?

But fince it was neither a fecret voice contrived by the cunning deceiver, nor an evil fpirit conjured up by her magic art, which pronounced the dread denunciation againft the trembling king, it muft have been Samuel himfelf, who revifited the earth to be the meffenger of thefe unwelcome tidings. Was he then called from his reft by the irrefiftible power of her incantations? Surely nothing can be more injurious to the perfections of the Almighty, than to fuppofe he would permit
mit

mit impious men, nay all the combined powers of darkneſs, to interrupt, even in the ſmalleſt degree, the peaceful reſt of his departed ſervants. Nothing can be more incongruous with reaſon than to imagine, that ceremonies however deviſed, or words however conſtructed and com-bined, can have any power to reanimate the mouldering duſt, and recal it from the ſilent manſions of the grave.* As ſoon may we expect to ſee ſpacious cities erected, noble foreſts called forth, and lofty mountains removed, by the potent ſound of cabaliſtic words. It muſt there-fore be by God's appointment that the departed prophet appeared. He was ſent to bring this ſevere and unwelcome meſ-ſage to Saul, as a rebuke for his preſump-tion, and a puniſhment for adding to his other ſins this flagrant tranſgreſſion of God's expreſs command.† Nor is ſuch a ſuppoſition repugnant to the divine pro-ceedings in ſimilar circumſtances. When the prophet Balaam practiſed inchant-

---

* See Farmer on Miracles, chap. iii. ſect. 3.
† Levit. xix. 26 and 31. And xx. 6.

B   ments,

ments, to obtain a favourable anſwer for
the Moabites, and a malediction againſt
the children of Iſrael, God continually
over-ruled him, conſtraining him to pronounce bleſſings inſtead of curſes.* When
king Ahaziah ſent to conſult Baalzebub,
the god of Ekron, whether he ſhould recover from his ſickneſs, the Lord ſent
Elijah to intercept his meſſengers, to re-
prove the king, and announce the unwelcome news of his certain death.† And
ſuch was his interpoſition in the caſe of
Saul. Saul came in hopes of obtaining
ſome grateful information from Samuel,
which he probably would have received
from the deſigning pretender to extraordinary powers, if God had not diſappointed both him and her, by ſending the real
Samuel to pronounce his awful fiat. Confounded by the unexpected ſeverity of this
ſentence, the king fell down in a ſwoon,
unable longer to ſuſtain the bitter agonies
of his mind.

* Numbers xxiii. and xxiv.
† 2 Kings i.

That

That the woman herſelf was greatly
diſappointed and deceived is clearly mani-
feſt from her behaviour, as ſoon as the
apparition preſented itſelf. Conſcious of
her own inability to call Samuel from the
dead, or to conjure up ſuch an appearance, no ſooner did ſhe ſee him, than ſhe
cried out with vehemence.* Struck with
ſuch an aſtoniſhing evidence of the divine
interpoſition, ſhe immediately concluded,
that the king alone could be the perſon
who applied to her, and ſhe exclaimed
with terror, " Why haſt thou deceived
me, for thou art Saul?" †

The ſuppoſition that it was Samuel
himſelf who appeared, is alſo plain and
natural, and conſonant to the ſtyle and

* The cauſe to which the Jewiſh Rabbins aſcribe her fright
is too ſingular and extravagant not to be mentioned: Becauſe,
ſay they, he did not appear in the uſual poſture of ghoſts
which are conjured up, with his head downwards and feet up-
wards, but erect as men ſtand when living. (Pool's Synop.
in locum.)

Joſephus attributes it to his venerable and majeſtic appearance; Θιασάμενον ἄνδρα σεμνον κỳ θεοπρεπῆ ταραάτlεται,
(Lib. 6. ch. 14.)

† Verſe 12.

tenor

tenor of the whole narration. Had it only been a perfonated Samuel, or only a familiar affuming Samuel's fhape and deportment, is it not probable, that the facred hiftorian would have given us fome intimation of it, and not have delivered the whole ftory precifely in the fame terms, as if the real Samuel had himfelf appeared?* The learned author of the book of Ecclefiafticus was clearly of this opinion. For he fays, " After his death " he prophefied, and fhewed the king his " end, and lifted up his voice from the " earth in prophefy, to blot out the " wickednefs of the people." †

To mention half the great authorities antient and modern, which might be

---

* The language of the narration is: " And the woman faw " Samuel." (ver. 12.) " Samuel faid to Saul." (ver. 15.) " Then faid Samuel." ver. 16, &c.) " And Saul perceived " that it was Samuel *himfelf.*" (ver. 14.) The Englifh tranflators, warped by their own preconceived notions, have omitted the word *himfelf,* which feems peculiarly directed againft the vulgar fuperftition of the power of witches over ghofts and fpectres. (Farmer on Miracles, ch. 4. fect. 2. p. 490.)

‡ Ch. xlvi. 20.

quoted

quoted in fupport of this opinion, would be trefpaffing too much upon your time and patience, but we muft not pafs over in filence the more weighty objections ad-vanced againft it.

When Saul afked the woman, "what faweft thou?"* She anfwered,—"I faw Gods *afcending* out out of the earth."†
Now, fay fome objectors, the righteous Samuel muft have been in a better place than the bowels of the earth, and confe-quently have rather been difcovered *de-fcending*. This objection, founded entirely upon the vulgar notions concerning the fituation of the places of future rewards

---

* Ver. 13.

† Or a God, viz, a perfon bearing the habit and dignity of a Magiftrate. ' That the word Elohim is applied to Judges and ' Magiftrates cannot be denied, See Exod. xxii. 8, 9, 28. ' Pf. lxxxii. 1, 6. Le Clerc and Patrick on 1 Sam. xxviii. 13. ' Dr. Chandler (in his life of David, p. 239) objects to the ap- ' plication of this plural Term to a fingle perfon; yet this ' Term is applied to Mofes, Exod. vii. 1. And it is certain ' that Saul did not underftand the witch as fpeaking of more ' than one perfon, for he afks, " what is his form?" And fhe ' explains her own meaning in the anfwer fhe returns to this ' queftion:—" An old man arifeth." (Farmer on Mir. Ch. 4. Sect. 2. p. 489. Note z.)

and

and punifhments, is too unimportant to
demand much of our attention. For can
it be of any great confequence from what
quarter Samuel appeared to make his ap-
proach? Befides, fo fudden and unexpected
was this vifit, that the woman in her violent alarm might eafily be miftaken.*

Again it is objected, the apparition com-
plains to Saul of being *difquieted* by him;†
but had it been Samuel no incantations
could have effected this, and if God had
fent him, he would not have complained.
Though Samuel could not be juftly dif-

* ' It does not appear that any magic rites were ufed, or
' that a moments time intervened between Saul's requeft, and
' Samuel's appearance. The Englifh tranflators have inferted
' the Particle *when*, ("And when the woman faw Samuel")
' without any authority from the original, and merely to fa-
' vor their own Prejudices.' (Farmer on Mir. Ch. 4. Sect. 2.
p. 487. Note s.) The paffage fhould therefore be read›
(V. 11, 12.) *Saul faid, bring me up Samuel. And the woman faw Samuel and cried with a loud voice.*

† V. 15. The judicious and learned Farmer (on Mir. Ch. 4.
Sect. 2. p. 492) tranflates this paffage, "why haft thou pro-
" voked me to rife up." Thus afcribinff his rifing up, not to
the Pythonefs or her magic art, nor ftrictly and properly to
Saul, but rather to the Prophet's indignation againft the
King.

pleafed

pleafed at being fent to execute the divine commands, yet as Saul's madnefs and prefumption were the caufe of his being called from his peaceful abode, did they not deferve fevere reprehenfion? And where was the impropriety of reproving Saul, who, though he could not compel Samuel's appearance, was undoubtedly the fole occafion of it?

But, fay our opponents, what reafon can be given, why God, who had refufed to anfwer Saul by his more ufual methods, fhould at laft declare his will to him by fuch fingular and unufual means?—Many of the difpenfations of Divine Providenc are enveloped in an obfcurity, which ou circumfcribed faculties cannot penetrate. That we are unable to give a fatisfactory reafon for any extraordinary interpofition of the Deity, can therefore be no valid argument againft the fact, if well eftablifhed. In this inftance however, the divine conduct may be accounted for. The Lord refufed to anfwer Saul, that being thus deferted, he might be awakened to a con

fcioufnefs

fcioufnefs of his crimes, and led to repent-
ance. But when inftead of rationally
obeying this admonition, he prefumptu-
oufly broke the law of his God, and applied to the pretended confulter of familiar
fpirits, the Lord embraced this opportunity of expreffing his juft refentment, and
denouncing that vengeance, which though
delayed, had not been forgotten. For by
this action, Saul had now filled up the
meafure of his guilt, as the Author of the
book of Chronicles clearly intimates.*
" So Saul died for his tranfgreffions,
" which he committed againft the Lord,
" even againft the word of the Lord,
" which he kept not; and alfo for afking
" counfel of one that had a familiar fpi-
" rit to enquire of it."†

Another moft material objection is advanced, which indeed would be decifive,

* 1 Chron. x. 13.

† In the Tranflation of the lxx. we find a remarkable addi-
tion to this Verfe; κ) απεκρίναιο αυτω Σαμυηλ ὁ προφήτης. And
Samuel the Prophet anfwered him." May not this be juftly
confidered as contributing to the fupport of our Hypothefis?

if

if once eftablifhed; that the predictions of this apparition were not true, and confequently could not have been delivered by God's meffenger, Samuel. For though it muft be acknowledged, that the things foretold did come to pafs in every particular, yet the language of the prediction was, "*to-morrow*, fhalt thou and thy fons be with me," though fome days might probably elapfe afterwards before the battle in Gilboa—As the learned in general agree,* that the word here tranflated, *to-morrow*, frequently fignifies, *very fhortly*, or hereafter, this difficulty is foon removed.†

* Univerfal Hiftory Vol. 4. p. 57. (Note P.)

† This interpretation of the word may be thought to render the whole prophecy fo vague and indeterminate, as to give it too much the air of an impofture; nor does there appear any neceffity for having recourfe to it, if we carefully attend to the circumftances of the Hiftory. Saul came to this female diviner by night, and having converfed with Samuel, and taken fome refrefhment, went away from Endor the fame night. Gilboa was not fo far diftant, as to render it impracticable for him to reach the Camp on the fucceeding day. The Jews in their computation of time reckoned the day from funfet to funfet, confequently the morrow or next day would not commence till after the funfetting, which fucceeded Saul's being at Endor. What therefore fhould prevent us from concluding, that the prediction, as it ftands in the common tranflation, was literally fulfilled?

C   But

But another immediately prefents itfelf: Is it not faid, "thou and thy fons
fhall be *with me?*" Was then the wicked
Saul to be claffed after death with the
righteous Samuel?—Suppofing the condition of a future ftate to be at all alluded
to here, might we not with equal propri-
ety afk; was no diftinction to be made be-
twixt the upright, pious Jonathan, and his
unjuft, ungodly father? This expreffion
therefore, *thou and thy fons fhall be with me,*
probably fignifies nothing more than this,
*thou and thy fons fhall like me be numbered
among the dead.**

I have now examined and endeavoured
to explain this remarkable ftory, which
has fo often been appealed to as incontrovertible fcripture authority for the vulgar
notions of conjuration and witchcraft.
And, I prefume, we are warranted in
concluding, from the arguments advanced; that it does not give the leaft

* By the lxx. this fentence is tranflated, " x) αυριον συ x) οἱ
" ηοι σε μετα σε πεσενlαι. And to-morrow thou and thy fons
" with thee fhall be flain."

support or countenance to such abfurd fuperftitions. One great obftacle is thus removed, which has prevented many from
believing, that thefe notions could be delufive. So far the ftrong evidence is
weakened, which has induced many to do
violence to their reafon, rather than dif-
believe what they imagined was fupport-
ed by unerring revelation. Some other
paffages of fcripture, which at firft view
appear to fanction thefe abfurdities, would
I am perfuaded, be found, upon a candid
examination, inimical to them. Several
arguments from reafon might alfo be advanced to prove fuch notions utterly void
of any real foundation. Though thefe I
am at prefent obliged to omit, yet a future day may perhaps afford me an opportunity of confidering them. And if at
laft fuch opinions fhould appear unable to
bear the teft of fair and free inquiry, with
what forrow muft we look back upon the
fate of thofe miferable wretches, who
have fallen the lamentable victims of fuch
fad delufion ?

Profiting

Profiting however by the example of Saul, let us endeavour to draw an ufeful leffon from this fingular part of his hiftory. Let it teach us, how impoffible it is to lay any fcheme of happinefs, unlefs favoured and fanctioned by God; how dreadful to have fo far provoked his indignation by our iniquities, as to be forfaken by him in our diftrefs : how tremendous to have him our enemy, when the awful hour of diffolution approaches! Let it alfo teach us, how defirable it is to enjoy his friendfhip and affection : how ineftimable a bleffing to have him for our guide and protector, when dangers and difficulties affail us! For, " if the Lord is on our fide, then need we not fear what man can do unto us;" fecurely fhielded by his Almighty wings, we may walk even through the valley of the fhadow of death without trepidation ! Confcious however that nothing but a pious and holy life can ever procure for us this pearl of ineftimable price, let us make religion our firft and principal care, as it is our greateft and moft important concern. Impreffed with

a

a due fenfe of the high value of this object, let us inftantly "give diligence to make
" our calling and election fure." And may
that being, who is all goodnefs and love,
affift and profper our humble and fincere
endeavours, fo that overcoming every
difficulty, and triumphing over every oppofition, we may finally obtain a glorious
and everlafting inheritance with the faints
in light.

SERMON

SERMON II.

1 Timothy iv. 7.

Refuse prophane and old Wives Fables.

A Strong predilection for the marve-
lous and extravagant has always
formed a diftinguifhed and ftriking fea-
ture in every rude, uncultivated mind.
Nor in any age has there been wanting knavery, ever ready and eager to take advantage of credulity and ignorance. Hence have
many idle and abfurd fuperftitions derived
their origin, and been moft induftrioufly
progagated amongft the ancient heathen,
during that long period of ignorance and
idolatry, which inveloped and obumbrat-
ed the major part of mankind. Much of
this darknefs has been already diffipated

by

by the pure light of the gofpel, which
has received no trifiing and inconfiderable
affiftance from that fpirit of rational philofophy, fo eminently difplayed in thefe
later ages. But almoft inconceivable is
the difficulty of eradicating a deep-rooted
fuperftition from the human mind, even
though its fallacy and abfurdity be pour-
trayed in the ftrongeft colours; efpecially
if the error has received the fanction of
remote and *venerable* antiquity. Yet the
difficulty of the work fhould ftimulate us
to redouble our exertions, and not fink us
in défpair; we fhould not be difcouraged
from fowing the feed with care and diligence, though the profpect of reaping the
defired harveft be diftant and uncertain.
Is not every effort to refcue mankind from
this dreary bondage, how weak and circumfcribed foever it be, juftly entitled to
the countenance and fupport of the candid and benevolent? Defirous of contributing, even the feebleft affiftance, towards
the advancement of fo defirable an event,
I have endeavoured, on a former occafion,
to fhew the inanity of the grand argument,

ment, ufually drawn from the hiftory of the Witch of Endor, in fupport of the vulgar notions of magic and witchcraft. My prefent intention is to make a few obfervations upon fome other portions of fcripture, which *may* be advanced in defence of thefe abfurdities, in order ftill farther to expofe the " bafelefs fabric" of fuch fuperftitions.

The oppofition made to Mofes and Aaron by the magicians of Egypt, conftitutes one of the moft fingular occurrences recorded in the pages of facred hiftory. For fome of the firft miracles, which the advocates of the chofen race performed, to prove themfelves the delegates of the Almighty, were immediately, imitated by thefe fervants of Pharaoh. Yet we find them afterwards obliged to defift from the conteft, and acknowledge themfelves unable to execute others, apparently not more wonderful.

And were miracles really performed in oppofition to the Sovereign of the Univerfe?

D

verfe? Let us carefully examine the principal circumftances, which accompanied
thofe extraordinary tranfactions, and from
thence endeavour to obtain a fatisfactory
anfwer to this important queftion.

God beheld his peculiar people, the
feed of Jacob, groaning under the fevere
yoke which the Egyptians had laid upon
them, and refolved to deliver them. For
this purpofe he fent Mofes and Aaron to
Pharaoh, to requeft that he would let the
Ifraelites go three days journey into the
wildernefs, to facrifice unto the Lord their
God. Satisfied with his own idolatrous
religion, the king faw no neceffity for
fuch a facrifice, and fufpecting it to be
only a pretext for getting out of his do-
minions, he ordered their labour to be
increafed, that they might have no leifure
for forming fuch dangerous projects. And
when, by their officers, they reprefented
their grievances to Pharaoh, inftead of
meeting with redrefs, they were infult-
ingly reproved for their idlenefs and dif-
affection. Groaning beneath fuch oppref-
fion,

fion, they directed their complaints againſt Moſes and Aaron, as the cauſe of their augmented burdens. In this dilemma Moſes applied to God, who again ſent him and his brother to Pharaoh, to repeat their demand in his name. The king now required of them a miracle, as a proof that they were indeed the delegates of God, and not mere pretending impoſtors. To ſatisfy him Aaron caſt his rod before him upon the ground, which was inſtantly transformed into a ſerpent. Immediately Pharaoh called together the wiſemen and forcerers of his court,* to try if

---

* The magi of antiquity were originally the prieſts of the gods, and the profeſſors of ſcience. They undertook to interpret dreams and prodigies, to foretel future events, and to perform many extraordinary things by the rules of their art, and their deep knowledge of the ſecret powers, and virtues of nature. Their art was built upon the general ſyſtem of Pagan theology, which deified all the powers of nature, and they pretended, by the uſe of proper charms and ceremonies, to be able to render the gods propitious to their deſires. They were frequently applied to by kings, particularly thoſe of Egypt and Babylon, where they flouriſhed moſt, and conſequently poſſeſſed conſiderable weight in the ſtate. To preſerve this influence, they were neceſſarily always ready to ſupply by artifice, whatever they wanted in ability.

Cicero de Divin.Lib. 1, Idem. de nat. Deorum,Lib. 2. Diogen. Laert. Lib. 7. Segm. 136, 137. Plutarch de placitis Philoſ. Lib. 2. c. 3. & aliis locis,

by

by their science and arts they could perform similar transformations. They at-
tempted and succeeded; nor were they less
fortunate in turning water into blood, and
in producing frogs; but bitter disappoint-
ment attended their future endeavours.

At the time of these events the Egyptians appear to have made some progress
in arts and learning; they had therefore
most probably discovered some of the wonderful operations of nature, which experimental philosophy displays. May we
not on this account reasonably conclude,
that there prevailed amongst them an opinion generally attendant upon the first
dawnings of knowledge and science; that
there are certain arcana or hidden quali-
ties in nature, by means of which many
surprising transmutations may be performed. The more enthusiastic of their
Philosophers would readily embrace such a
pleasing delusion; and the more designing
would willingly cherish a notion, by which
their influence and power would be so effectually promoted. Is it not probable
that it was some such an opinion as this,
which

which induced Pharoah to affemble the Egyptian Philofophers,* in order to examine, through their means, whether the works of Mofes were really miraculous, or whether he only took advantage of his extraordinary knowledge of natural arcana,† when he pretended to be directed and affifted by the finger of God. If fuch were the King's views, need we wonder

* To fuppofe that Pharoah fent for the Magicians to try, whether the God of Ifrael was really more powerful than the Gods of Egypt, and confequently able to compel him to difmifs his people, accords not with the fundamental principles of pagan theology. For though it reprefents the Gods as frequently efpoufing different parties, fome being inimical while others are propitious, yet it never encourages it's votaries to expect that'one Deity vill protect them from the vengeance of another, but rather exhorts them to labour, to appeafe the angry and adverfe Gods by facrifices and fupplications. Mofes did not appeal to his miracles, as evidences of the fuperiority of Jehovah over the Egyptian Deities; but as proofs that he alone was God of the Univerfe. And the Magicians did not endeavour to counteract or controul Mofes, but merely to imitate him, that they might thus invalidate the credentials he produced in fupport of his divine commiffion. In this light the fubject is confidered by Jofepnus, Antiq. Jud. Lib. ii. Chap. 13. See alfo Shuckford's Connection, Vol. II. p. 457, &c. &c. Farmer on Mir. Ch. iii. and Ch. iv. Sect. 1.

† Many of the ancients imagined that Prodigies, Divinations, &c. might be procured without the Deity's interpofition by the ufe of natural means, and by attention to certain difcipline and rules of Art; as appears from Cic. de Div. Lib. i. and Plutarch, Lib. de defectu Oraculorum.

that

that his heart fhould be hardened, when he faw his own magicians able to imitate the advocates of the Hebrews; or can we deem it furprifing, if, even after *they* gave up the conteft, he fhould ftill feel an inclination to attribute the fubfequent performances of Mofes to his fuperior fkill.

Was there really any occult fcience, any hidden powers of nature, by which the Magicians were enabled to produce fuch extraordinary effects without fupernatural affiftance?—In an age like the prefent, when experimental philofophy is fo accurately and extenfively cultivated, no one can for a moment withhold his negative to this queftion.

Did they play their parts as jugglers and cheats, pretending to do what they did not, and impofing upon the credulous Pharaoh by Sleight and Artifice?" Would not this have given Mofes and Aaron too good an opportunity of detecting their impofture, and expofing them moft effectually to the King and his attendants? Befides, if we fuppofe them capable of fubftituting ferpents, or blood, or

frogs,

frogs, with ſuch adroitneſs, as to exhibit
the appearance of a tranſmutation, will
it not be difficult to aſſign a ſufficient reaſon, why they were not able to ſubſtitute
lice and flies and locuſts with equal ſkill
and ability ?*

Were

---

* Since writing and preaching the above Sermon, further
reflection upon the ſubject, and attention to the arguments of
others (particularly of the late learned and elaborate Mr.
Farmer, in his excellent work on miracles) have induced the
Author to believe the performances of the Magicians, to be
nothing more than the effects of artifice and colluſion. But
for ſeveral reaſons he deems it almoſt a duty that the Sermon
ſhould appear, as nearly as poſſible, in it's original form, and
rather than make ſuch a complete alteration of it, to place in
a Note the principal arguments which have cauſed this change
in his opinion, referring thoſe who wiſh for further information on the ſubject to the judicious writer above-mentioned.
(Ch. 4. Sect. 1.)

To imagine that God himſelf gave unexpected ſuccefs to the
Magicians, is it not to make him act in oppoſition to himſelf,
working ſome miracles to confront the authority of Moſes, at
the ſame time that he was working others to eſtabliſh it ?
If Jehovah thus required Pharoah to do and not to do the ſame
thing, with what juſtice could he afterwards puniſh him ſo ſe-
verely for refuſing to diſmiſs the Iſraelites?

The appellations by which Moſes deſcribes his oppoſers fa
vour this Hypotheſis. For the words, which our tranſlators
have rendered *Sorcerers* and *Magicians*, ſignify rather *Juglers*,
who delude the eyes of the ſpectators by ſleight and cunning,
and *interpreters*, who undertake to explain things obſcure and
difficult

Were they then aſſiſted by any evil
Dæmons, who performed at their requeſt
what

difficult. (Vid. Buxtorf and Pagnin, in voc. et Johan. Cler
in Gen. xli. 8.)

Theſe Magicians would naturally conclude, that Moſes and
Aaron were only profeſſors of the ſame Arts with themſelves,
and knowing how ſtrongly the prejudices and intereſt of Pharoah would bias him in their favour, they would not heſitate
to contend for the palm of ſuperior ſkill, before ſo partial a
judge. Whatever was done by theſe Egyptians, Moſes aſ-
cribes to their *inchantments*, or their *covert Artifices and
crafty juglings*, as the words more properly import, (See the
comments of B. Kidder, B. Patrick, and Le Clere, on
Exod. vii. 11.)

The phraſe made uſe of by him, in deſcribing their performances, does not aſſert a perfect conformity between his own
works and theirs, but only a general ſimilarity, or perhaps in
its ſtricteſt ſenſe, merely their " *attempting* ſome imitation of
" Moſes: for it is uſed even when they failed in their at-
" tempt. *They did* SO—to bring forth lice but they could
" not." (Ch. viii. 18.)

But why were they not equally ſucceſsful in producing lice,
as in their previous feaſts of Dexterity?—In the former in-
ſtances they knew before hand what they were about to undertake, and had time for preparation. Pharaoh did not ſend
for them at firſt, till after Aaron's rod had been transformed
into a ſerpent, and previous notice had been publicly given
of the two prior plagues ; (Ch. vii. 15, 17, and viii. 1. 4.) but
the execution of the third inſtantly ſucceeded the command ;
(Ch. viii. 16, 17,) the Magicians had therefore no time for
previous contrivance. Beſides, the minuteneſs of the ſubſtan-
ces, with which they had to do, rendering them imperceptible

at

what human power was unable to accomplifh?—The author of all things has regulated univerfal nature by fixed and fettled laws, and the very effence of every miracle confifts in a violation of thefe laws. But how can their operation be for a moment interrupted by any power lefs than that, which originally conftituted them? And is it not the height of folly and impiety, to afcribe fuch ability to any other being than that infinite God, by whom and in whom all things confift.

But if no affiftant familiar could be able to perform real transformations, might he not prefent fuch delufive appearances before the eyes of Pharaoh and his fubjects, as to make them imagine they faw the rods of the magicians changed into ferpents, frogs produced, and water converted into blood, though no fuch things were in reality performed?—To exhibit thefe delufive appearances would be no lefs wonderful, no lefs a breach of the ordinary

at a diftance, neceffarily fubjected them to fuch near and clofe infpection, as made it almoft impoffible for the moft dexterous fubftitution to efcape undetected.

E

laws

laws of nature, than the abfolute comple-
tion of the real miracles. And if we fuppofe the performances of the magicians
to be mere deceptions of the fenfes, what
arguments can we advance to refcue the
actions of Mofes from a fimilar imputati-
on? If the works appeared to be performed, the fpectators could have no certain rules by which they might diftinguifh
a real miraculous effect from a falfe delufive appearance.

But if the Egyptian Magicians had no
myftical arts, no pre-conftructed rules by
which they could enfure themfelves fuccefs, is it not furprifing that they fhould
make any attempts, and ftill more aftonifhing that thefe attempts fhould prove
fuccefsful?—We have no reafon to fuppofe
that the King, when he called them together, entertained any *very* fanguine expectations, that they would be able to
perform the tafk enjoined. We have
more authority for concluding that, actuated by a full perfuafion of the exiftence
of many occult powers in nature, he
wifhed

wifhed to try what Art could effect, in order to know whether the works of Mofes
were the refult of human ingenuity, or interpofitions of divine power. What abfurdity is there in imagining, that the
Magicians themfelves were not free from
fome tincture of the fame unfounded notions? The Priefts of Baal, in the days of
Elijah, could have no grounds for think-
ing that their incantations would draw
down the wifhed for fire from Heaven;
yet, incited by enthufiafm and rage, they
tried every extravagant artifice with aftonifhing perfeverance from morning until
evening.* Why then might not thefe
Egyptians in a fimilar manner try every
fanciful experiment, though perfectly un-
warranted in any expectation of fuccefs,
by any thing they had before feen. An
event, favourable as their moft fanguine
wifhes could afpire to, was beftowed upon
their attempts by the Almighty, for the
promoting and accomplifhing his defigns.
One of thefe probably was the admini-
ftring occafion for more and greater miracles, that his chofen people might be

* 1 Kings xviii. 26, &c

imprefled

impreffed with a more lafting idea of his
power, and be thereby induced to pay a
more willing and fteady obedience to his
commands. By means of Pharoah's obftinacy the Majefty and Power of Jehovah
were without doubt more amply difplayed.
God himfelf declares,* "And in very deed
" for this caufe have I raifed thee up, for
" to fhew in thee my power, and that my
" name may be declared throughout the
" earth." The fuccefs of the Magicians
appears to have even exceeded their own
expectations : They did not know the extent of their own power, if indeed it be
not ridiculous to conceive them endowed
with any. For had they proceeded upon
certain rules of Art, they would have
known before trial what they ought to
attempt, and what they would be able to
accomplifh. But their unfuccefsful endeavours prove their ignorance in this refpect; and how little they were fatisfied
with their own performances, is fufficiently evinced by the readinefs with which
they embraced the firft opportunity, af-

* Exod. Ch. ix. 16.

forded

forded them by the failure of their attempts, to acknowledge that Mofes was directed and affifted by power from on high.

On a review of the preceding arguments, are we not warranted in concluding,* That the fage philofophers of Egypt, who oppofed the deliverers of Ifrael, were not enabled to perform miracles by the knowledge of any arcana of nature, or by the rules of any dark and occult fcience ; and that the furprifing fpectacles they exhibited, were not performed by any agency of the inhabitants of the fpiritual world.

But if the two moft remarkable relations, which the facred writers have tranfmitted to us, do not eftablifh thofe abfurd notions which fuperftition has taught, and ignorance believed for fo many ages, with what hopes can their defenders appeal to fcripture for their fupport?

* Whichfoever of the two hypothefes we adopt.

In

In the law of Mofes this command is delivered: " There fhall not be found " among you any one that maketh his fon " or his daughter to pafs through the fire, " or that ufeth divination, or an obferver " of times, or an inchanter, or a witch, " or a charmer, or a confulter with fa- " miliar fpirits, or a wizzard, or a ne- " cromancer." * Again, " A man or a " woman that hath a familiar fpirit, or " that is a wizzard, fhall furely be put " to death : they fhall ftone them with " ftones; their blood fhall be upon them."† And again, " Thou fhalt not fuffer a " witch to live." ‡ But, it may be ar- gued, Why fhould the divinely infpir- ed legiflator have enumerated thefe as crimes, and denounced fuch fevere pu- nifhment againft them, if no one was pof- feffed of fuch extraordinary and deteftable powers? We need not infift upon the de- viation from the ftrict meaning of the ori- ginal, into which our tranflators have been drawn by the difference of cuftoms and opinions, and by their ftrong preju-

* Deut. xviii. 10, 11. † Lev. xx. 27. ‡ Exod. xxii. 18.

dices

dices in favour of the vulgar errors of their own times.* Setting thefe afide, a moment's reflection upon the caufe and intent of the Mofaic inftitution will fhew, how little neceffity there is for us to do violence to reafon, in complaifance to the letter of thefe denunciations. God had feparated the children of Ifrael from the reft of mankind, to preferve amongft them the knowledge and worfhip of the one Supreme, in the midft of that deluge of polytheifm and idolatry, which was wide extending its deftructive ravages over the face of the globe. Every inftitution of the law of Mofes was therefore intended for this purpofe, and directed to the promotion of this defign, as

* See Le Clerc and Patrick's Com. on the feveral texts. Shuckford's Connec. Vol. 2. p. 395. and Scot's Difcovery upon the refpective Words.

The tranflation of the Bible now in ufe, was made at the particular requeft of James the Firft, who, a few years before, had written his book on *Dæmonologie.* We cannot help acceeding to the opinion of Dr. Hutchinfon, who imagines, that the tranflators were induced to adopt phrafes favourable to the vulgar fuperftitions, by their Reverence for the *profound* learning and judgment of their Sovereign. Hutch. on Witchcraft, ch. 14. p. 225.

its

its primary object. God did not wish to make them a nation of enlightened and accurate philosophers, nor did he endeavour to correct one speculative principle, which did not necessarily beget immoral and idolatrous actions. The Israelites were just come up out of Egypt, where they had imbibed a strong propensity for those superstitious notions and practices, to which that country was so remarkably enslaved. Attachment to these necessarily drew along with it a degree of affection for those idolatrous rites, with which many of them were so closely connected, as to render their separate existence impossible. These superstitious observances were therefore punished with this exemplary severity, in order to block up this inlet to idolatry, and to preserve the chosen seed of Jacob from going astray after strange gods. Accordingly we find all these offences ranked in the same class with the detestable sacrifice of their children, offered by the worshippers of Molock to that horrid idol. Amongst a nation

tion fo ready to give credit to their pretenfions, there muft always be found de-
figning men, who would arrogate to themfelves extraordinary powers. Thefe muft
neceffarily be confidered as infamous fe-
ducers of the people, as men who were
erecting the ftandard of rebellion againft
their fovereign, and throwing down the
altars of their god. For, by the covenant
made with the children of Ifrael, Jehovah
was conftituted both their God and King.
Confiftently therefore with the whole tenor
of this inftitution, all thefe pretenders to
fupernatural qualifications were as juftly
punifhed, as if abfolutely poffeffed of the
attributes they claimed.

Such is the fupport which the facred
writings afford to the fuperftitious belief
of more than human powers, in reputed
witches and converfers with familiar fpirits. If reafon be confulted, every light
it affords ferves ftrongly to point out the
folly and extravagance of the notion. In
fpite then of the general reception, which

F   this

this once favourite opinion has met with in the days of ancient ignorance, it may be defervedly claffed amongft thofe " pro- " phane and old wives fables," which the apoftle exhorts us to reject, as inimical to the pure religion of the gofpel.

Is it not a lamentable reflection, that for ages thefe abfurdities fhould have been che- rifhed with the greateft care, as valuable truths; and that many innocent creatures fhould have fallen victims to the general bigottry and madnefs ? But how far more fhocking to obferve,that many of thofe,who were peculiarly called by their fituation to labour for the inftruction and enlighten- ing of mankind, have ever been the moft zealous defenders of error and abfurdity? But let *us* profit by their example, and ftrenuoufly endeavour each in his pro- per fphere to difpel the mifts of igno- rance and fuperftition from the minds of thofe around us, fenfible that the removal of any foolifh error is one ftep towards eftablifhing true and pure religion upon a

firm

firm and fold bafis. And let us not only difcountenance and refufe every prophane and old wives fable; but attending to the fubfequent advice of the apoftle, " Let " us diligently exercife ourfelves unto " godlinefs; for godlinefs is profitable " unto all things, having promife of the " life that now is, and of that which is " to come."*

* 1 Tim. iv. 7, 8.

SERMON

SERMON III.

ECCLES. i. 9.

There is no new Thing under the Sun.

TO trace this memorable obſervation of the wiſe preacher through its full extent, to examine its juſtice, and diſplay its truth, is a taſk I ſhall at preſent decline. It is my intention to conſider the text ſolely with reference to that one ſubject, which the peculiar circumſtances of the day more immediately recommend to our conſideration. Having, on the preceding occaſions, examined the two moſt extraordinary narratives, and alſo other paſſages of the Old Teſtament, with a view to ſubſtantiate

tiate this propofition; that the facred
authors give no fupport or countenance
to the vulgarly received notions of witchcraft, I fhall now endeavour to fhew, that
thefe cannot have received in more recent
times any fufficient and incontrovertible
fanction. God from the beginning has
bound univerfal nature by fixed and per-
manent laws, nor has he ever fuffered
them to be for a moment interrupted or
fufpended by any created being in oppofition to his will. The power of working
miracles he has referved to himfelf alone,
and to this have his favoured meffengers
always appealed, as the peculiar and indifputable evidence of his interpofition.
The moft remote ages furnifh us with ex-
amples of pretenders to extraordinary
powers, who impofed upon the credulity
and ignorance of the undifcerning; and
the boafted abilities of more modern times
have been equally the offspring of fuperftition and knavery. For in this refpect,
" there is no new thing under the fun."

The

The powers of man have increafed, and may probably yet increafe beyond what we at prefent can conceive, by the increafed knowledge of the efficacy of natural caufes; yet it is impoffible for thefe caufes, though under the moft fkilful direction, ever to produce miracles, or effects repugnant to the fettled laws of the univerfe. That any human being is, or ever can be, able by his own unaided power in the fmalleft degree to interrupt the regular courfe of nature, none, I imagine, will be found hardy enough to maintain. All modern advocates for vulgar miracles, are therefore obliged to have recourfe to the agency of more potent fpiritual beings, who have covenanted to fubmit themfelves to the commands of feeble mortals.* To point out an adequate reafon for their entering into fuch a compact, would require more than common fagacity ; and admitting the agreement to exift, what evidence have we of their ability to perform their part of the extravagant engagement ?

* King James's Dæmonologie, Book 2. ch. 2. Bodin des Sorciers, lib. 1. ch. 2. Scot's Difcovery, book 3. ch. 1.

If

If we apply to reason, what information does she afford us ? Reason points out to us, but one omnipotent Being, who is capable of acting every where, and in what manner soever he pleases, whose omnipotence is the only adequate cause we can discover of every miraculous effect. That there are created beings superior to man seems highly probable, but the exact extent of their power, reason cannot discover ; that they are confined to their own proper sphere of action, appears most agreeable to the general œconomy of nature. The close connection between the different orders of beings, in this system of ours, does not prove any necessary communication between the inhabitants of other systems, and this lower world : Nor can we argue from our mutual dependence upon each other, that they have any more power over us than we have over them. It is reasonable to suppose, that spiritual beings have powers superior to those of men; but we cannot justly conclude from thence, that this material world is equally subject to their influence.

The

The general idea we form of them is, that they are void of folidity. Then how can they act upon matter by impulfe, or what neceffary connection can we difcern between their volition and the motion of material beings? * Is it not inconfiftent alfo with the goodnefs of God, that he fhould fuffer the laws of nature to be controuled at the will of any created being? For then the harmony and regularity of both the natural and moral world muft foon be confounded, and confequently the defigns of infinite power and wifdom for the benefit of his creatures, be completely defeated. Befides, experience does not afford us any fatisfactory proofs that they at prefent do, or ever have performed miracles in this lower world. †

If we confult revelation, does it afcribe to them any fuch faculties?—The bleffed

---

* The late Dr. Ifaac Watts has treated this fubject, with his ufual ingenuity and acutenefs, in his Philofophical Effays on various fubjects, Effay 6th.

† See more on this fubject in Farmer on Miracles, ch. 2. Dr. Douglas's Criterion, and Dr. Hutchinfon on Witchcraft.

G   angels

angels are reprefented as God's minifters, delivering no meffages to man but what they firft receive from him, and never interfering in the affairs of our fyftem, but in obedience to his exprefs commands. For " they are all miniftering fpirits do- " ing his commandments, and hearken- " ing unto the voice of his words."* And if good angelic beings, who enjoy the approbation and favour of their Creator, have no power of working miracles at their pleafure, no dominion over mankind, is it not folly to imagine thofe capable of fuch wonderful exertions, who by their tranfgreffions have incurred the divine difpleafure ? God has not enlarged their powers in reward of their difobedience, but " has caft them down into hell ; and " referved them in everlafting chains, † " under darknefs, unto the judgment of

* Gen. xix. 13. Pf. ciii. 20, 21. If. vi. 1, &c. Dan. viii. 15, 16. Heb. i. 14. and Ch. ii. 5. Rev. xix. 10.

† Into Tartarus (ταρταρωσας) How much foever we may be at a lofs to form a precife idea of the place here referred to, we cannot reafonably imagine it to be their kingdom, but rather their everlafting prifon.

the

" the great day." * " The fcripture
" never afcribes to the devil the ability of
" revealing fecrets, foretelling future
" events, or working miracles; never
" guards mankind againft being deceived
" by the outward effects of his miracu-
" lous power or infpiration; neceffary as
" fuch a caution would have been, had he
" been able to infpire prophecies, and to
" work miracles; and earneftly as it
" warns againft a lefs danger, the pre-
" tences of men to divine miracles and
" infpiration, when they are not fent and
" affifted by God." † In fhort, in almoft
every page of the facred volume is this
important truth inculcated; That " Je-

---

* 2 Pet. ii. 4. Jude 6. The commonly received interpretation of thefe paffages has been adhered to, as the only one
which affords any fupport to the notion, that evil fpirits ever
interfere in terreftrial affairs. But it would be difingenuous
not to acknowledge my affent to the opinion of thofe who contend, that by the ἄγγελοι here mentioned, the apoftles did
not mean *evil fpiritual beings,* who rebelled in heaven againft
their almighty Sovereign; but rather the *meffengers,* who,
being fent from the camp of Ifrael to view the land of Canaan,
" brought up an evil report of the land," thus feducing the
people to murmur againft Jehovah, and diftruft his promifes.

† Farmer on Mir. ch. 3. fect. 1. p. 153.

G 2   " hovah

" hovah he is God in heaven above, and
" upon the earth beneath, there is none
" elfe ;" and " he only doeth wondrous
" things ?" *

But, admitting that any created being
is at liberty to controul the courfe of nature, without the exprefs authority and
commiffion of the Almighty, what rule
can we have for diftinguifhing between
the wonderful works of thefe petty rulers,
and the interpofitions of the Supreme?
They are both alike appeals to our fenfes,
both equally furpafs our conceptions; and
are both entitled to equal regard. Behold, then the dreadful confequences!
Thofe miracles, to which we are accuftomed to appeal as infallible evidences
of the truth, *may* have been exhibited in
fupport of pernicious error; nor can we
prove that Mofes was not a lying prophet,
and Jefus Chrift a vile profligate impoftor.

* Deut. iv. 39. Pf. lxxii. 19. compare 2 Sam. vii. 22.
Pf lxxxvi. 10. cxxxix. 1—12. If. xlv. 5, 6, 7, 18, 21, 22.
Ch. xliii. 10—13. Jer. xxxi. 35.
Farmer on Miracles, ch. 3. fect. 5.

Is

Is it not impious to imagine that God hath left his creatures fo open to be feduced by every lying vanity, fo liable to fall into the fnare of every wicked deeiver? Befides, the very foundation of filial reverence and pious obedience, towards our eternal Father and King, muft be entirely overwhelmed. For if any other beings can fufpend the laws and difturb the order of the univerfe, is it not incumbent upon us to worfhip them, to appeafe their wrath and obtain their favor? And upon what can God found his claim to our exclufive homage? Has not fuch an opinion been in all ages fatal to true piety, has it not given birth to an endlefs train of ancient pagan idolatries, and modern antichriftian fuperftitions? But if thofe extraordinary performances, which vulgal credulity believes and ignorance too generally records and trembles at, are found to exceed the capacities of created beings, muft not all fuch idle ftories be void of any real foundation? For furely it is moft impious to fuppofe, that God himfelf can ever interfere in an unufual manner,

ner, merely to gratify the wanton caprice or angry refentment of a weak, if not a wicked child of mortality.

If we had no other reafon for doubting the truth of thofe ftories, which the abettors of witchcraft propagate, our faith muft certainly receive a violent fhock, by only confidering to whom thefe unufual faculties are in general afcribed. To wretches bending beneath the load of years and infirmities, too often oppreffed by the additional burden of pinching poverty, and in their appearance remarkable for nothing but the diftreffing fpectacle of fqualid mifery which they exhibit. Had the Devil or his fubjects the powers afcribed to them, and had witches authority to command and direct their efforts, they would furely firft of all require relief from their diftreffes, if not a plentiful fupply of every article of terreftrial luxury and enjoyment. Is it not abfurd to imagine, that any one fhould enter into a compact with the Prince of darknefs, to do his errands of mifchief, without receiving any

any better return for their labours, than poverty here and mifery hereafter? It is certainly not enough that they fhould fometimes make nightly excurfions to fome diftant region, there to revel upon imaginary dainties;* dainties imaginary as their renowned witchcrafts, which only have exiftence in the idle fears of the credulous, and the difeafed imagination of the melancholy Hypocondriac.†

Againft fuch ftrong reafoning, what do the advocates of thofe grofs fuperftitions oppofe? A tedious train of abfurd or fanciful facts. If any foolifh experiment has appeared to be attended by the expected event, how often has it been conftrued into undeniable ocular demonftration of guilt? If a poor creature, irritated by the infulting petulancy of fome infolent and unfeeling wretches, and unable through

* Dr. Hutchinfon on Witchcraft, Ch. 13. p. 211,

† For an account of the extravagances which authors have gravely related, concerning thefe meetings of witches, and concerning their Sabbaths, we refer the curious to Bodin de Sorciers, Liv. 2. Chap. 4. 5. Scot's Difcovery, Book 3. Ch. 2. 3. King James Dœmonologie, Book 2. Chap. 3.

infirmity

infirmity or want, to obtain more fubftan-
tial redrefs, has been driven to vent the
paffion of her foul in imprecations, and
fome misfortune has foon afterwards happened to any of them, this has frequently
been received as incontrovertible proof of
her diabolical machinations. If any one,
poffeffing an imagination crowded with notions of witchcraft, has had the misfortune
to be afflicted with any unufual diforder,
how ftrongly has he been inclined to attribute it to the agency of fome affociate
of the infernal powers? Let this imagination once acquire firm root in the mind,
and in vain will you endeavour to eradicate it by the force of reafon. Soon does
memory, from the recollection of fome
peevifh altercation, furnifh an object of
fufpicion, and from that moment every
action is viewed through a falfe medium :
occurrences otherwife indifferent now af-
fume the form of prefumptions, and fancied evidences are tortured into undeniable proofs. Thus upon pretexts the moft
frivolous and abfurd, has the peace, nay
too often the lives of our fellow-creatures
been

been facrificed. Frequently has interefted knavery thrown an indelible ftigma upon innocence, and fometimes purfued its poor devoted victim even to deftruction.

But one difficulty, may our adverfaries triumphantly fay, yet remains unremoved. Did not many confefs their guilt? Have there not been numerous inftances of thofe who have openly acknowledged their abominable witchcrafts, and impious league with the Dæmons of darknefs? With forrow, not unmingled with fhame, do I confefs that the number of fuch has indeed been confiderable. Alas! poor human nature, how frail, how imperfect are all thy vaunted excellencies! How do I abafhed, behold thine honour levelled in the duft! What poignant grief muft a-rife in the breaft of the humane, when contemplating the effects of an imagina-tion difordered and depreffed by melan-choly! It has exalted poor infane wretches in their own idea to royal and imperial dignity, and caufed fome even to arrogate to themfelves the fublime title of the Mef-

H   fiah:

fiah:* others it has depreffed beneath humanity, while they have confidered themfelves as brutes, inanimate bodies, or beings compofed of glafs. But if a difeafed
fancy can work fuch ftrange and deplora-
ble effects, can we be at all furprifed, that
perfons whofe imaginations had long
brooded over the notions of witches and
witchcraft, fhould acquire a full conviction
that they were themfelves poffeffed of
fuch extravagant powers? This falfe affo-
ciation being once completely formed, it
would make the fame impreffion upon the
mind, as if it were perfectly true. How
eafily then, would they be perfuaded, that
they had performed fuch acts as their
imagined qualifications enabled them to
do, and how readily would they acknowledge them? And why fhould it excite our
aftonifhment that many miferable creatures, harraffed by importunities and
overcome by difgraceful and iniquitous

---

* There is no neceffity for an elaborate refearch into hiftory
to prove the ftrong effects of a difordered imagination, when our
own times furnifh us with a Richard Brothers and his ferious
fupporters.

tortures,

tortures, have been reduced to the confeffion of crimes, which they never could
be able to commit.*

But if thefe fuperftitious notions are
falfe and groundlefs, whence had they
their firft origin, and how did they acquire
fuch deep root in the minds of men?
—When we confider that thefe opinions
firft fprang up in the dark ages of heathen
antiquity, of which fcarce any record has
furvived the ravages of time, we muft acknowledge this to be a queftion of fome
difficulty; yet a little reflection may perhaps afford us fomething like a fatisfactory
anfwer. Fear is one of the ftrongeft paffions of the human mind, and capable of
preferving the moft complete and perma-
nent influence over it. Upon this
bafis all the idolatrous rites of the
ancient Pagan nations appear to have
been erected; all their religious cere-

---

* Will not all thefe confeffions be invalidated by applying
to them this excellent rule, Confeffio rei impoffibilis non eft confeffio fanæ mentis; the confeffion of an impoffibility is not the
confeffion of a found mind?

monies

monies being intended to deprecate the anger, rather than merit the favor of their Gods. This flavifh fear was encouraged by the crafty priefts, becaufe it gave them a more unlimited influence over the people; and connived at by the civil rulers, becaufe it difpofed the fubject to fubmit more tamely to abfolute tyranny. The former, as engaged in the immediate fervice of the Gods, claimed the privilege of a more intimate and familiar acquaintance with them, which claim the people might be induced to acquiefce in by fome remaining tradition of God's intercourfe with the firft patriarchs. On this foundation they built their pretenfions to divination and other extraordinary performances. By a monopoly of the little learning of their times, and the help of numerous impoftors and juggling tricks, they maintained their own and the reputation of their Gods. The *facred* profeffors of thefe arts generally met with protection and encouragement from the ftate, on account of their important fervices to thofe in power; but inferior pretenders, who,

wifhing

wifhing to prey upon the weaknefs and errors of their fellows, made large additions to the idle tales, by which the credulous multitude was amufed and mifled, were publicly condemned in almoft every nation without being exterminated.* By thefe means fuperftition was heaped upon fuperftition, till at laft that immenfe fabric of abfurdities was raifed, which has fo long held the ignorant in bondage, and which as yet time has not been able to deftroy.

The apoftle Paul has warned us againft giving credit to fuch " profligate venders of lies." "Now the Spirit fpeaketh ex-
" prefsly, that in the latter times fome
" fhall depart from the faith, giving heed

---

* Tacitus calls thefe, Genus hominum potentibus infidum, fperantibus fallax, quod in civitate noftra vetabitur femper et retinebitur. Hift. Lib. 1. Jamblichus, in his treatife upon the myfteries of the Ægyptians, Chaldæans and Affyrians, gives us reafon to conclude, that the jealous Priefts, ftigmatifed thefe intruders into their province as men rejected by the Gods, and abandoned to the fociety of evil Dæmons, by which connexion they became like their affociates, full of malice and mifchief.

" to

" to feducing fpirits and doctrines of de-
" vils;* fpeaking lies in hypocrify," or
rather, *thro' the hypocrify of liars*, who
ftrive to fupport their deadly errors† by
falfe legendary miracles, whom every pious chriftian fhould avoid as men " who
" having their confciences feared with an
" hot iron."‡

All fuch notions appear to have
been treated by the firft propagators
of chriftianity as wicked fables; and in one
of the early chriftian councils at the city
of Ancyra they received a fevere cenfure,
and the believers of them were con-

---

* δαιμονιων, of Dæmons, that is, the fouls of men deifyed after death.

† Of the divinity and worfhip of deadmen *(canonifed faints)*
afcribing to them the power of working miracles, and making
them a fort of mediators between God and men; an impious
abfurdity which had its origin with the pagan Priefts and Philofophers, who afcribed to fuch Dæmons the immediate infpection and government of this lower world. Plutarch de defectu Orac. Plato in Sympos. Apuleius (de deo Socrat.)
fays, Cuncta cæleftium voluntate, numine et auctoritate, fed
dæmonum obfequio et opera et minifterio fieri arbitran-
dum eft.

‡ 1 Tim. iv. 1, 2.

demned

demned as infidels and worfe than pagans.*
Neverthelefs, when heathen philofophy
began to be grafted upon chriftianity, the
purity

* This council, holden in the year 314 at Ancyra, the metro-
polis of the province of Galatia, was compofed of 18 bifhops,
from whofe decrees the following curious extract is recommended
to the perufal of our readers: Illud etiam non eft omittendum,
quod quædam fceleratæ mulieres, retro poft fatanam converfæ,
dæmonum illufionibus & phantasmatibus fubductæ, credunt et
profitentur fe nocturnis horis cum Diana paganorum dea, vel
cum Herodiade & innumera multitudine mulierum, equitare
fuper quafdam beftias, & multa terrarum fpatia intempeftæ
noctis fpatio pertranfire, ejufque juffionibus velut dominæ obe-
dire, & certis noctibus ad ejus fervitium evocari.   Sed utinam
hæ folæ in fua perfidia periiffent, et non multos fecum in infi-
delitatis interitum pertraxiffent.   Nam innumera multitudo,
hac falfa opinione decepta, hæc vera effe credit, et credendo
a recta fide deviat, et in errore paganorum revolvitur, cum
aliquid divinitatis aut numinis extra unum Deum arbitratur &c.
Omnibus itaque publice annuntiandum eft, quod qui talia et
his fimilia credit, fidem perdit.   Et qui fidem rectam in domino
non habet, hic non eft ejus, fed illius in quem credit, id eft,
Diaboli.   Nam de Domino noftro fcriptum eft; Omnia per
ipfum facta funt.   Quifquis ergo credit poffe fieri aliquam cre-
aturam, aut in melius aut in deterius immutari, aut transfor-
mari in aliam fpeciem vel fimilitudinem, nifi ab ipfo creatore,
qui omnia fecit, & per quem omnia facta funt proculdubio in-
fidelis eft & pagano deterior. (Concil. general. per Binnium,
tom. 1. p. 275.)   This alfo ought not to be omitted, that certain wicked women, led aftray after Satan, and feduced by the
deceptions and delufions of Dæmons, believe and profefs that
they ride in the night upon certain beafts with the heathen
goddefs Diana, with Herodias and women without number,
and travel over an immenfe tract of country ; that they obey
her

purity of the gofpel became contaminated, and the innocence and integrity of it's teachers corrupted. Ignorance again fpread it's dominion far and wide, and the chriftian priefthood, forfaking the fteps of their divine mafter, deviated into the paths of their idolatrous predeceffors. Like them they ftrove to eftablifh their empire over the minds of the people: inftead therefore of labouring to extirpate, they continued to nourifh thofe abfurdities, which paganifm had bequeathed to

her commands as their miftrefs, and on particular nights are called out to wait upon her. But it would be well if they perifhed alone in their perfidy, and did not draw many along with them into the fame deftructive abyfs of infidelity. For a vaft multitude, deceived by this falfe notion, believe thefe things, and by fo believing fall from the true faith, and relapfe into the error of Paganifm, when they fuppofe that there does exift any fpecies of divinity or deity befides the one Supreme God.—It is therefore neceffary to declare unto all, that whofoever believes fuch things forfakes the faith. And he that poffeffes not the true faith in the Lord, is none of his, but rather his, in whom he believes, that is, the Devil's. For it is written concerning our Lord, all things were made by him; whofoever therefore believes that any creature can be made, or even altered for the better or the worfe, or fuffer any transformation in fpecies or appearance, except by the Creator himfelf, who made all things, and by whom all things were created, he without doubt is an infidel, and worfe than a pagan.

mankind.

mankind.* They attributed a power of working miracles, to evil angels, whom they confidered as the real objects of ancient heathen worſhip, and perſecuted their fancied human aſſociates as enemies of God. With what injuſtice and inhumanity this proceſs was conducted, the edicts of the Popes and the acts of the inquiſitors ſufficiently teſtify.† To the united force

I of

---

* The various ſects of Gnoſtics early introduced into the chriſtian world the old heathen doctrine of the two principles, the good and the evil; Manes or Manichæus grafted upon chriſtianity a large portion of the Perſian mythology, and his opinions were in a great meaſure embraced by Priſcillian and his followers. The council of Bracara in Spain, holden in the year 563, cenſured theſe extravagant notions concerning the power of the Devil or evil principle. In one of their decrees, they anathematiſed all thoſe who believe the Devil can make any creature, or ſo much as raiſe ſtorms and tempeſts by his own authority. Si quis credit, quod aliquantas in mundo creaturas Diabolus fecerit, & tonitrua & fulgura & tempeſtates & ſiccitates ipſe Diabolus ſua auctoritate faciat, ſicut Priſcillianus dixit, anathema ſit. Neverthelefs many of theſe abſurd notions gained ground in the ſucceeding ages of ignorance and degeneracy, and became the baſis of all thoſe extravagant ſuperſtitions, which afterwards received the ſanction of the higheſt eccleſiaſtical authority.

† Popiſh ignorance and ſuperſtition having now attained the zenith of their power, Pope Innocent VIII. in the year 1484,

iſſued

of fuperftition and knavery, multitudes
fell a lamentable facrifice. This intol-
rant fury was gradually checked by the
advancement

iffued his memorable bull, directed to the Inquifitors of Almain, &c. empowering them to fearch out and caufe to be
burnt, all fuch as were guilty of the *herefy* of witchcraft.
The tenor of this bull will beft appear from a fhort extract :
Innocentius Epifcopus, Servus Servorum Dei, &c. Sane nuper
ad noftrum non fine ingenti moleftia pervenit auditum, quod
in nonnullis partibus Alemannæ, &c. complures utriufque fexus
perfonæ, a fide catholica deviantes, cum Dæmonis, Incubis &
Succubis abuti, ac fuis incantationibus, carminibus & conjura-
tionibus, aliifque nephandis fuperftitionibus & fortilegiis, ex-
ceffibus, criminibus & delictis, mulierum partus, animalium
fœtus, terræ fruges, vinearum uvas & arborum fructus, nec-
non homines, mulieres, pecora, pecudes & alia diverforum ge-
nerum animalia, vineas, quoque pomaria, prata, pafcua, bla-
da, frumenta & alia terræ legumina perire, fuffocari & extin-
gui, facere & procurare, ipfosque homines, mulieres, jumenta,
pecora, pecudes, diris tam intrinfecis quam extrinfecis dolori-
bus & tormentis afficere & excruciare, ac eofdem homines ne
gignere, and mulieres ne concipere, virofque ne uxoribus,
et mulieres ne viris actus conjugales reddere valeant,
impedire. Fidem præterea ipfam, &c. abnegare, &c. Nos igi-
tur, &c. auctoritate Apoftolica tenore præfentium ftatuimus,
&c. hujufmodi inquifitionis officium exequi, ipfafque perfonas,
quas in præmiffis culpabiles repererint, juxta eorum demerita
corrigere, incarcerare, punire & multare, &c. invocato ad
hoc, fi opus fuerit, auxilio brachii fecularis. (vid. Jac. Spren-
ger, Malleum Malef.—Barth. Spin. de ftrigibus, c. 3.) Innocent,
bifhop, a fervant of the fervants of God, &c. We have heard
not without great forrow, that in many parts of Almain, &c.

great

advancement of learning, and the reforma-
tion of religious error, till at length a final
period has happily been put to such abo-
I 2

minable

great numbers of both ſexes, forſaking the catholic faith, abuſe
their own bodies with devils of both ſexes; and with inchantments, charms, conjurations, and other wicked ſuperſtitions
and ſorceries, exceſſes and crimes, deſtroy and cauſe to be ex-
tinguiſhed, the births of women, the fœtuſes of cattle, the
fruits of the ground and of the trees, and even men, women,
cattle and other kinds of animals; they blaſt vines, fruit-trees,
paſtures, corn-fields, and other productions of the earth; they
afflict and torment men, women, cattle and other animals with
dreadful internal and external pains and tortures, and deprive
men and women of the powers of procreation, &c. They
alſo renounce the faith, &c. We therefore, &c. by our
Apoſtolical authority, appoint by theſe preſents, &c. to execute the office of inquiſition, and to correct, impriſon, puniſh,
fine, &c. according to their demerits, thoſe perſons whom they
ſhall find guilty of the crimes aforeſaid, &c. calling in for this
purpoſe, if it be neceſſary, the aſſiſtance of the ſecular arm.

The idle ſuperſtitions of witchcraft being thus methodiſed and
ſanctioned by the infallible head of the church, the fury of
eccleſiaſtical perſecution was now let looſe againſt all the fancied aſſociates of the dæmoniacal powers, and extended its horrid ravages over countries conſecrated to the Prince of Benevolence and Peace. In the year after the promulgation of
this bull, the inquiſitor Cumanus burnt 41 poor women for
witches, in the country of Burlia. (H. Inſtit. p. 105.) And
Aliciat in his Parerga ſays, that one inquiſitor burnt 100 in
Piedmont, and proceeded daily to burn more till the people
roſe againſt him and chaſed him out of the country. A few
years

minable public facrifices, though the torch of private perfecution, is too often lighted at the yet remaining embers of fuperftitious credulity.

May true knowledge fpread abroad its benign, its virtuous influence, till every foolifh fuperftition, every antichriftian bigotry is totally eradicated from the mind of man. And let us labour with all our powers to haften this defirable event; yet, contemplating the great miftakes which others have

years afterwards, more than 500 (fays the Jefuit Delrio in his preface, p.3.) were executed in the city of Geneva, in the fpace of three months. In the year 1524, 1000 were burnt in the diocefe of Cumo, and 100 per ann. for feveral years together, (Barth. Spin. cap. 12.) Many more inftances of thefe fuper-ftitious cruelties are given by Dr. Hutch, ch. 2.

In the hands of a bigoted, ambitious Clergy, and a fuperftiti-ous, fervile Laity, thefe extravagant criminations became an excellent engine for promoting the views of the popifh church. The Priefts of that church eagerly propagated the opinion, that all thofe, who oppofed their ufurpations and errors, were leagued with the Prince of darknefs, and that herefy and for-cery were indiffolubly united. (Delrio difq. mag.) By this means many poor Waldenfes and other Proteftants, fuffered for the imputed fin of witchcraft, when their abominable dif-fent from the *holy* Church of Rome was their real crime. Truth indeed obliges me to confefs that fome Proteftants have re-torted the accufation, and charged fifteen Popes in fucceffion from Silvefter II. to Gregory VII. with being Magicians.

fallen

fallen into, let us proceed with caution, and with diffidence in our own abilities. Becaufe we have been enabled to advance further in the inveftigation of truth than our anceftors, let us not imagine that we are endowed with any additional perfections. Confcious that our judgment is circumfcribed, and our reafon thwarted by the fame infirmities and paffions, ("for there is no new thing under the fun") let us cultivate an affectionate regard for the prejudices and infirmities of others. Are we ourfelves ftrong? It is our duty to bear with the weak. Have we been able to overcome the delufion of any error? It is incumbent upon us to inftruct others with fincerity, with meeknefs, with gentlenefs and goodwill. And may the God of truth direct all our inveftigations, and profper all our endeavours, to the advancement of his glory and the happinefs of our fellow-creatures; fo that, at the clofe of our probation here, we may look back upon our paft conduct with fatisfaction, in joyful confidence that we fhall receive his approbation.

SERMON

SERMON IV.

PSALM xxxi. 6.

I have hated them that regard lying Vanities ;

but I truſt in the Lord.

WHEN laſt I appeared before you, I endeavoured to add to what had already been advanced, every obſervation, which appeared to be of any conſiderable importance upon that intereſting ſubjeĉt, to which the peculiar circumſtances of our aſſembling more immediately directed our attention. Being therefore unexpectedly called upon once more to addreſs you from this place, on the ſame extraordinary topic, pardon me, if I indulge a confident hope that you will eaſily

be

be induced to fpare your cenfures, though this difcourfe fhould have little or nothing of novelty to recommend it. While however we in fome meafure re-trace the path we have already troden, fome hitherto fcarcely perceived object may perhaps prefent itfelf to our view, which may tend to increafe and eftablifh our averfion to the lying vanities of vulgar fuperftition, and induce us with the Pfalmift to *hate* all thofe who regard them.

To *hate* a fellow-creature! Who that has an heart poffeffing the fmalleft fpark of humanity, does not fhrink from the idea with a facred horror? And could the infpired fervant of God applaud, and by his own example recommend fuch inveterate perfecuting malevolence? Surely this is impoffible.—The language of the man after God's own heart appears to have been this,* " When

---

* This Pfalm appears to have been compofed in the midft of fome preffing difficulty, or rather immediately after fome extraordinary deliverance. Why fhould we not refer it to fome of thofe critical fituations, to which David was reduced, when flying from the perfecuting malevolence of Saul, when fo great was his danger, that without a fignal interpofition of Providence, his efcape feemed almoft impoffible ?

" involved

'involved in difficulties and diftreffes, I
'have not relied upon vain, fuperftitious
'obfervances, I have not confulted any of
'the various tribe of prophane diviners;
'fuch practices I have always regarded
'with abhorrence and the obfervers of
'them with deteftation. But my confi-
'dence has always been placed in the
'living God, and to him alone have I ap-
'plied for direction.' He could not poffibly be ignorant of the denunciations,
which the law pronounced againft the infamous practicers of idolatrous incantations, how then muft he have been offended
at all thofe, who difobediently confided in
fuch foolifh delufions; how muft he have
burned with indignation againft all thofe
knavifh impoftors, who preyed upon the
credulity of their weak brethren. For
fuch he muft neceffarily have confidered
all the pretenders to fupernatural power
and knowledge, when he ftigmatifed all
their boafted performances as "lying vanities." And every page of Scripture,
when candidly examined, breathes the
fame fpirit. It is in the fame ftrain of

K   pointed

pointed reprobation, that God addreffes his chofen people: "Hearken not ye to "your prophets, nor to your diviners, "nor to your dreamers, nor to your in- "chanters, nor to your forcerers :—For "they prophecy a lie unto you."* By what ftronger term could the exercifers of fuch arts be branded than that of lyars; or in what more pointed manner could their practice be marked as the fole off- fpring of human fraud and artifice? It muft be acknowledged, that viewing them through the medium of prejudice and miftranflation, many fincere and not weak believers have conceived the facred pages to fpeak a different language. How lau- dable therefore every effort to draw afide the veil which obumbrates their immacu- late fplendor, and purge them from thofe blots, with which infidelity has, with too great appearance of reafon, exultingly re- proached them?

To what has been, with this defign, laid before you on former occafions, one

* Jer. xxvii. 9, 10. Compare Ch. xxix. 8, 9.

ufeful

uſeful obſervation may without impropriety be added. The ſcriptures more intent upon making men good than learned,
have always accommodated their diction
to the conceptions and prejudices of thoſe
addreſſed. They give indeed to vain
boaſters the appellations of prophets, diviners, magicians, witches, and the various other epithets, which ignorance has
ever beſtowed, or knavery aſſumed. But
this is no more a poſitive proof of their
poſſeſſing anſwerable powers, than the
corporeality of the Deity is evinced by
ſuch expreſſions as, *the hand of God;* or
the modern ſyſtem of natural philoſophy,
which reſts on the adamantine baſis of de-
monſtration, is overthrown by Joſhua's
ſaying, *the Sun ſtood ſtill.**

---

* A careful examination of thoſe paſſages of Scripture,
where ſorceries and witchcrafts are mentioned, will be ſufficient
to convince the unprejudiced, that nothing more is meant
thereby, than ſome of the various modes of divination, practiſed by the idolatrous heathen, thoſe vain attempts to dive
into futurity, which tended to alienate the heart from the true
God. Compare 1 Sam. xv. 22, 23. 2 Kings, ix. 22. 2 Chron.
xxxiii. 6. Iſ. xlvii. 12, 13. Jer. xxvii. 9, 10, Ezek. xxi.
21, 22. Mich. v. 12, 13. Nahum iii. 4.

It

It would be almoft culpable not to embrace this opportunity of making a remark upon the account of Simon of Samaria, which is tranfmitted to us in the Acts of the Apoftles. " But there was a " certain man called Simon, which before " time in the fame city ufed forcery, and " *bewitched* the people of Samaria, giving " out, that himfelf was fome great one. " And to him they had regard, becaufe " that of a long time he had *bewitched* " them with forceries."*

Thofe excellent men, to whom we are indeed exceedingly indebted for our tranflation of the facred records, involuntarily drawn into an error by their own preconceived notions, have here reprefented as fupernatural effects, thofe *juggling tricks*, by which the artful impoftor *aftonifhed* the ignorant Samaritans. For the original words imply no more, and it is rather fingular, that they fhould in one verfe have rendered the fame verb

* Ch. viii. 9, &c.

bewitched,

bewitched, * which in another they have only tranflated *wondered,* when defcribing the effect, which the real miracles of Philip had upon Simon himfelf. " Then " Simon himfelf believed alfo, and when " he was baptized, he continued with " Philip and *wondered,* beholding the mi- " racles and figns which were done."

The principal evidence which reafon furnifhes us with, in this curious and fingular inveftigation, has already been examined. The general conclufion which we have endeavoured to eftablifh, would be confiderably ftrengthened by a candid examination into the circumftances of thofe cafes, which have received the fanction of different courts of juftice, as indifputable proofs of diabolical guilt. Thefe

* εξιϛημι. It may not be improper to tranfcribe from the original, verfes, 9, 11, & 13. Ἀνὴρ δέ τις ὀνόμαϊι Σίμων, προϋπῆρχεν ἐν τῆ πόλει μαγεύων καὶ ΕΞΙΣΤΩΝ το ἔθνος τῆς Σαμαρείας, λέγων εἶναί τινα ἑαυτὸν μέγαν.-----Προσεῖχον δὲ αὐϊῶ, διὰ το᾽ ἱκανῷ χρόνῳ ταῖς μαγείαις ΕΞΙΣΤΑΚΕΝΑΙ αυτύς.-----Ο δὲ Σίμων καὶ αὐτὸς ἐπίϛευσε, καὶ βαπϊισθεὶς ἦν προσκαρτερῶν τῳ Φιλίππῳ· θεωρῶν τε σημεῖα καὶ δυναμεις μεγάλας γινομένας, ΕΞΙΣΤΑΤΩ. Vid. Smidium in Act. viii. 13.

again

again we might compare with others, where impofture has been detected, or an heated and deranged imagination difcovered.* This however, would be a tafk much more tedious than ufeful, and we may be fufficiently convinced of their general abfurdity and iniquity, by confidering the nature of the evidence, and the rules of judging, which fuperftition has in fuch cafes· ufually had recourfe to. Some of thefe are indeed too fanciful and foolifh to bear a ferious recital ;† but the iniquity

---

* See Scot's Difcovery, Dr. Hutchinfon on Witchc. Ch. 4. & 15.

† A man may reafonably doubt, whether he fhould more indulge his indignation or laughter, to find fuch filly tefts efteemed adequate proofs of guilt, as, the accufed parties not being able to repeat the Lord's Prayer without miftakes; being outweighed by the Church Bible; fwimming with thumbs and toes tied acrofs; being unable to fhed tears; having the Devil's Mark, an apparent fore rendered infenfible of pain, and which might appear like the bite of a Flea; or feeret Teats, (like Warts or Moles,) at which their imps were allowed to fuck, an abfurd notion almoft peculiar to this Country, where feeding and rewarding imps was made a capital Felony: thefe imps might appear, if their coming to take their accuftomed repaft was watched, in the fhapes of Cats, Dogs, Rats, Mice, Birds, Flies, Toads, Fleas, &c. they might alfo be kept in

pots

iniquity of others will fcarcely allow them
to be paffed over unnoticed. While trials
for the crime of witchcraft were fafhiona-
ble, it was deemed juft to apply tortures
to the accufed wretches, or to afflict and
harrafs them by want of food and priva-
tion of reft, till from the difordered and
diftracted mind fomething was extorted,
which appeared like a confeffion of guilt.
And if, when reft and food had reftored
the underftanding, this were denied, it
was conftrued into a proof of *diabolical* obftinacy rather than a prefumption of innocence. On thefe trials the teftimony of
perfons was received, whofe infamous
characters rendered them incapable of
being admitted as witneffes in other cafes.
Againft one accufed of any one particular
act of forcery, any matter might be admitted in evidence, however foreign to the fact
in queftion, even though it had occurred
at the moft diftant period. If the afflicted

pots or other veffels, were they would ftink deteftably ; fo that
if any poor accufed wretche's houfe emitted a difagreeable fmell, it
was a fure fign that imps were kept there, though thefe nafty
elves could not be found. See Dalton's Country Juftice.—
King James's Dæmon.—Sad. debel—Bodin, &c.

party

party fancied he faw his fuppofed tormen-
tors, it was efteemed ftrong proof againft
them: even the ill fame of a perfon's anceftors was accounted a reafonable caufe
of fufpicion; and to crown all, it was received as a maxim, that the eftablifhed
practices of courts of judicature, when
taking cognizance of this diabolical crime,
were not to be examined and canvaffed by
reafon. Before courts conftituted upon
thefe principles, and judges acting by
thefe rules, what accufed perfon could
have the fmalleft hopes of vindicating his
innocence? For there prejudice muft tri-
umph over reafon; fancy ufurp the throne
of judgement; fufpicion and proof, accufation and conviction be completely confounded. Yet to the refult of fuch idle
and iniquitous inveftigations alone, can
the advocate of thefe fuperftitious vanities
appeal, in fupport of their real and folid
exiftence. And with what heartfelt forrow muft we add, for fuch weak and
wicked imputations, have thoufands of
our fellow-creatures felt the agonizing
fcourge, perifhed on the accurfed tree,

or

or breathed out their spirit in the consu-
ming flames. Alas! such are the baneful
effects of superstition.

View the progress of this pernicious
spirit, under whatever form and at whatever period, it has intruded itself amongst
the sons of men, and it will ever be found
the enemy of humanity, virtue and
piety. It's inevitable tendency is to alienate the heart from God, to establish a
dependence upon idle ceremonies and
vain observances. Wherever this hateful
tyrant has been able to erect her throne,
pure and undefiled religion has been driven into exile and oblivion. How is this
lamentable truth confirmed, by the united
testimony of every page of Pagan history!
How is it confirmed, by a dismal view of
those long protracted years of ignorance,
when papal superstition triumphantly
tyrannized over the western world, al-
most extinguishing the pure light of revelation, and expelling divine truth from
the regions of christendom! But to past
times we have scarce occasion to appeal,

L   if

if we do but contemplate with attention the prefent ftate of mankind. The knowledge and love of the true God appear juft fo far to have advanced their power and influence, as ignorance and fuperftition have been chafed from the field. But what bitter fenfations muft arife in every philanthropic breaft, to fee how little progrefs has yet been made in the important work of enlightening and reforming mankind? Is it not almoft enough to unnerve our efforts, when we confider the mighty labours which are yet to be atchieved before this defirable end is accomplifhed? Is it not almoft fufficient to fink the moft refolute perfeverance in defpair, when that tenacious obftinacy is contemplated, with which long eftablifhed abfurdities are cherifhed, as moft valuable treafures? Who can, without poignant emotion, behold intereft and ambition inceffantly, and but too fuccefsfully, labouring to preferve the empire of ignorance over the minds of the multitude? But furely the fublimer motives of humanity and benevolence muft be ftrangers to the breaft of him, who

who can refuſe to lend his zealous aid, towards the extirpation of all " lying vani- " ties," if he but conſiders their baleful in- fluence. Would he lead mankind to the ſervice of God, here let him commence his labours. Would he erect on earth the manſion of that " godlineſs, which has " the promiſe of the life, that now is, " and of that which is to come," here let him lay his foundation. The ſlave of bi- goted prejudice, as well as the ſubject of impure paſſion, cannot poſſeſs that child- like ſimplicity, with which the apoſtle ex- horts us, to receive " the ſincere milk of " the word, that we may" be nouriſhed, and " grow thereby." He muſt be void of that kind, long-ſuffering charity, with- out which, all his profeſſions are but " ſounding braſs, and a tinkling cymbal." This univerſally benevolent principle is incompatible with that perſecuting ſpirit, which can haraſs a brother for opinions ſake, or deſtroy him for fancifully im- puted crimes.

L 2 But

But fuch a fpirit is the fure offspring of fuperftition, that defolating fiend, which, under the falfe title of wars of religion, has deluged the earth with blood, facrificed by whofe tyranny the fmoke of the army of martyrs has afcended to heaven. This, this is the dæmon, which can rob us of our reafon, and fteel our hearts againft the fympathifing calls of humanity, can arm us with the mad folly of brutes, and the unfeeling malice of furies. Then let man, in every ftation, and in every clime, raife his arm againft this hideous enemy, let him exert all his powers to chafe this dire deftroyer from the face of the earth. Yes, let him banifh this parent of " lying vanities, and truft in the " Lord."

Methinks I hear fome calm, cool objector fay,—What, eradicate all at once thofe fuperftitious notions, which ferve to awe the ignorant, and frighten them into their duty, and will they not wildly rufh into the paths of difobedience?—With what painful conviction of the imperfec-
tion

tion of human nature, muft every one,
acquainted with man, acknowledge this
ungrateful truth? Through a long feries
of revolving ages, fuperftition nourifhed
by ignorance, and too often cultivated by
knavery, has wide extended its dominion
over the minds of men. With the bulk
of the human race, if we entirely deprive
them of this reftraint, we leave the will
uncontrouled, and the underftanding a
void, ready to be feized and tyrannized
over by the firft invading paffion,

Then fhould we ftrive to eradicate by
gradual culture, and the introduction of
more pure and exalted motives, what it
would be unfafe inftantly to expel. It is
thus that we muft lay the foundation of
all true regard and confidence in the
great fupreme, a confidence fpringing
from love and gratitude towards a graci-
ous benefactor, not an homage generated
by a fearful dread of an omnipotent Lord.
For it is not as an arbitrary tyrant, that
our God would be flavifhly obeyed ; but
as a beneficent Father, that he would be
                                    willingly

willingly honoured. He is defirous that
all his creatures fhould look up to him,
as the being whofe providential care and
tender mercies pervade and preferve the
univerfe, that they fhould place their dependence upon him, and not give to another any portion of that refpect and honour, which is due to him alone.

The natural offspring of prevailing fuperftition is infidelity. Of the truth of
this the prefent times afford us a lamentable example. Where ignorance and fear
once ruled fupreme, there has rafh philofophy but too fuccefsfully planted prefumption and atheifm, 'Tis the diffufion
of pure and folid knowledge, which alone
can preferve us from the dominion of thefe
oppofite tyrants. How fhould this confi-
deration increafe our zeal and ftimulate
our endeavours! The immediate fphere
of our action may be circumfcribed, but
our exertions will not on that account be
entirely loft. In that circumfcribed fphere
let us labour to root out every fuperftitious

tious lying vanity, and plant pure religion
and unfophifticated truth in its ftead.

How charming, how enlivening to the
foul, to gaze upon the dawning beams of
opening light, to behold them irradiate
that difmal gloom of intellectual darknefs,
which long overwhelmed the millions of
mankind: How fupremely pleafing, to
view them wider and wider fpreading their
invigorating influence : How rapturoufly
tranfporting, to contemplate the fplendef-
cent profpect of pure and perfect day!

> " Power fupreme !
> " O everlafting King ! to thee we kneel,
> " To thee we lift our voice ;"—

O fpread thy benign, thy vivifying light
over the dwellings of the fons of men;
difpel the yet impending mifts of ignorance and fuperftition : And, O preferve
us from the difmal gulph of infidelity and
atheifm; Let thy truth run and prevail
glorioufly ; let pure, celeftial wifdom
overfpread the earth as the waters cover
the

the fea!—Then fhall millions kneel before thee with grateful and enraptured hearts; then fhall they rejoice to fing the praifes of thee, their Benefactor, their Father, and their God: Then fhall this vale of tears be filled with the manfions of joy and gladnefs, and become a blifsful fore tafte of thofe regions, where thy faints, crowned with unfading glory and felicity, furround thy throne with never ceafing hallelujahs !

F I N I S.

THE MOST

STRANGE AND ADMIRABLE DISCOVERIE

OF THE

THREE WITCHES OF WARBOYS,

Arraigned, convicted, and executed,

At the laſt ASSIZES at HUNTINGDON,

For the bewitching of the Five Daughters of

ROBERT THROCKMORTON, Eſquire,

And divers other Perſons,

Withſundrie Divelliſh and grievous Torments:

AND ALSO FOR THE

Bewitching to Death of the Lady CRUMWELL,

The like hath not been heard of in this Age!

LONDON. 1593.

S U C H is the title-page of that curious narrative, an abridgement of which is here ſubmitted to the reader's peruſal. As far as could conveniently be done, the words of the original have been adopted, and are diſtinguiſhed by a ſingle in-

M   verted

verted comma. The fingularity of the
fubject, rendered it almoft impoffible to
forbear interfperfing a few obfervations,
but it did not appear neceffary to point
thefe out by any particular mark of diftinction ; the difcerning reader will eafily
difcover them, and readily accede to them
if juft.

   ' About the 10th of November 1589,
' Miftris *Jane*' one of the daughters of
' the faid Mafter *Throckmorton*, being neere
' the age of ten years, fell upon the fodaine
' into a ftrange kind of ficknefs, the man-
' ner whereof was as followeth. Sometimes
' fhe would neefe very lowde and thicke
' for the fpace of halfe an houre together,
' and prefently as one in a great trance
' and fwoune lay quietly as long : foone
' after fhe would begin to fwell and heave
' up her belly, fo as none was able to keep
' her down : fometime fhe would fhake one
' leg, and no other part of her, as if the
' paulfie had been in it ; fometime the
' other : prefently fhe would fhake one of
' her armes, and then the other ; and foone
after

' after her head, as if she had been inflict-
' ed with the *running paulsie*.' In this
manner she had continued to be affected
for several days, but without any suspicion
of witchcraft, when old *Alice Samuel* came
to visit the sick child, and sat down by the
side of her in the chimney-corner, having
a black knit cap on her head. This the
child soon observed, and pointing at her,
exclaimed, ' Grandmother, looke where
' the old witch sitteth; did you ever see
' one more like a witch than she is? Take
' off her blacke thrumb'd cap, for I cannot
' abide to looke on her.'

The child still growing worse rather
than better, her parents sent her urine to
Cambridge, to Dr. *Barrow*, ' a man well
' known to be excellent skilful in phisicke,'
who, after repeatedly trying the effect of
his prescriptions, without success, ven-
tured to suggest, ' that he had some expe-
' rience of the malice of some witches, and
' he verily thought that there was some
' kind of sorcerie and witchcraft wrought
' towards this child.' This suggestion,

M 2   however,

however, did not make any deep impreffion upon the minds of her parents,
' until one juft month after, (the very day
' and houre almoft obferved),' when two
more of their daughters were feized with
the fame malady, and complained in the
fame manner of *Mother Samuel.* Soon afterwards the youngeft daughter was feized,
and laft of all the oldeft was reduced to the
fame fituation though ftill more feverely
handled than her younger fifters; they all
however agreed, in placing all their afflictions to the account of old *Alice Samuel.*

It may not be fuperfluous juft to mention, that the fame charge was brought
againft this old woman by the fervants of
Mr. *Throckmorton*, who, to the number of
fix, were at different periods afflicted in
the fame manner as his daughters.

To the fceptic this may appear but
weak evidence, but what objection can he
make to the clear proof of guilt, which
was furnifhed from the following experiment? In the month of February, fucceeding

ceeding the commencement of this *lament-able tragedy*, thefe children were vifited by their uncle *Gilbert Pickering*, Efq. who, on his firft arrival at *Warboys*, found them all ' very well as children could be.' He then went, with others, to the houfe of mother *Samuel*, ' to perfuade her to come ' to fee and to vifit the faide children ;' but this reafonable requeft fhe refolutely refufed,—undoubtedly from a confciouf-nefs of her guilt, and a fear left fome clear proof of it fhould be exhibited. But upon Mr. *Pickering*'s threatning to compel her, if fhe refufed to go of her own accord, fhe at laft complied, and was accompanied by her daughter *Agnes Samuel*, and one *Cicely Burder*, her fufpected confederates in this abominable witchcraft. No fooner had fhe ' entered the hall, where three of the ' childred were ftanding by the fire per-' fect well, but at one moment, they all ' fell down upon the ground ftrangely ' tormented, fo that if they had been let ' lie ftill on the ground, they would have ' leaped and fprung like a *quicke pickerel*, ' *newly taken out of the water*.' Almoft
immediately

immediately one of them, *Jane Throck-morton* was taken up, carried into another room, and laid upon a bed, the covering of which fhe foon begun to fcratch, re-peatedly crying out, ' Oh that I had her, Oh that I had her.' Mr. *Pickering*, fur-prized at this, fetched mother *Samuel*, (' who came as willingly as a beare to the ' ftake'), to the child's bed-fide, and de-fired her to put her hand to the child's, but fhe refufed, though encouraged by the example both of Mr. *Pickering*, and others, whofe hands, however, ' the child would fcarce touch, much lefs fcratch.'

At length, ' without any malice to the ' woman, confidence or opinion in fcratch-' ing, (only to tafte, by this experiment, ' whereto the child's words would tend) ' he took mother *Samuel*'s hand, and thruft ' it to the child's hand, who no fooner felt ' the fame, but prefently fhe fcratched her ' with fuch vehemence, that her nayles ' brake into fpiiles, with the force and ' earneft defire fhe had to revenge.' In the midft of her rage, Mr. *Pickering* co-vered

vered the old woman's hand with his own, yet the child would not ſcratch his hand, but ' felt eagerly for that which ſhe miſſ- ' ed,' and mourned bitterly at the diſap- pointment. All this time not only her eyes were cloſed, but her face was alſo turned from Mr. *Pickering*, and his companions, and hid in the boſom of the perſon who held her down upon the bed.—How then was it poſſible for her, to diſtinguiſh the hands preſented to her, except by the di- rection of the evil ſpirit, which poſſeſſed her? Unleſs indeed we have recourſe to the *extravagant* opinion, that *ſhe could be directed by the motions and whiſperings of the company about her, or could be able to diſtin- guiſh by the touch, the ſhrivelled hand of a old woman from that of any other perſon.*

The preſence and agency of an evil ſpirit were evinced by repeated occur- rences. For generally when ever prayers commenced before theſe children, the wicked ſpirit would ſhew its reſent- ment, by tormenting them, but would ' inſtantly be quiet, as ſoon as prayer end- ' ed;

' ed ;' even grace before or after meat
it would feldom hear with patience, or
fuffer family prayer to pafs over in peace,
though the children were removed into
another room. The fame was the cafe,
when ' any one read the Bible, or any
' other godly book, before them ;' and
not unfrequently at the mention of ' any
' word that tended to God, or godlinefs,
' the fpirit raged all one as if any read or
' prayed by them.' One particular inftance
the reader will excufe our inferting. When
one of thefe children was in her fit, a perfon prefent ' chanced to afk her, or rather
' the fpirit in her : Love you the word of
' God ? whereat fhe was fore troubled and
' vexed.   But love you witchcraft ?   it
' feemed content.   Or love you the Bible ?
' again it fhaked her.   But love you Pa-
' piftrie ? it was quiet.   Love you prayer ?
' it raged.   Love you the Maffe ? it was
' ftill.   Love you the Gofpel ? againe it
' heaved up her bellie : fo that what good
' thing foever you named, it mifliked ; but
' whatfoever concerning the *Pope's paltrie*,
' it feemed pleafed and pacified.'   At the
fame

fame time this evil fpirit, or fpirits, would allow thefe children, with apparent plea-fure, ' to play at cards, or any other fool-' ifh game,' with fome *one* they might pick out of the company, and whom they would fee and converfe with, though un-able to fee or hear *any one elfe.* For fuch was the fingular variety of their afflictions, that fometimes they would be totally in-fenfible, fometimes they would be able to fee and hear, but not to fpeak; fometimes to hear and fpeak, though not to fee; and fometimes to fee and converfe with parti-cular perfons, though completely infenfi-ble of the prefence or converfation of any other perfon. Nor were the modes of reliev-ing them from their diftreffing fituation lefs fingular; if carried into the open air, to fome particular place, or in fome par-ticular direction, they would recover; but if returned to their former place or fituation, they would immediately relapfe. When in their fits, the children them-felves, *(or rather the fpirits)* would fre-quently predict their own recovery, at a certain time, upon being conveyed to a

N   certain

certain place, or upon the performance of a certain ceremony, *which predictions were uniformly verified by the event.*—The unbelieving fceptic may perhaps confider fome of thefe circumftances, as ftronger indications of *human* delufion or knavery, than of extraordinary *fpiritual* agency. But fhould we corroborate the fact by half the curious inftances the original furnifhes us with, this narrative would be fwelled to an extravagant fize; and more *important* matter claims our attention.

After thefe children had, for fome time, fuffered in this extraordinary manner, in the month of March, 1590, they were vifited by the Lady of Sir *Henry Cromwel:* ' She had not long ftaid in the houfe, ere ' they all fell into their fits,' *(an occurrence which invariably took place whenever any ftrangers came to fee them)* ' and were fo ' grievoufly tormented, that it pitied that ' good Ladies heart to fee them : Where- ' upon fhe caufed mother *Samuel* to be ' fent for;' and, taking her afide, fhe ' charged her deeply with this witchcraft,
' ufing

' uſing alſo ſome hard ſpeeches to her,
' but ſhe ſtifly denied them all, ſaying,
' That Maſter *Throckmorton*, and his wife,
' did her much wrong, ſo to blame her
' without cauſe.' Lady *Cromwel*, unable
' to prevail with her by good ſpeeches,
' ſodainly pulled off her kercher, and ta-
' king a paire of ſheeres, clipped off a
' locke of her haire, and gave it privily
' to Miſtreſs *Throckmorton*, together with
' her hair-lace, willing her to burn them.'
Perceiving herſelf ſo ill uſed, ſhe ſaid to
the Lady : ' *Madam, why do you uſe me*
' *thus ? I never did you any harm as yet.*'
' The ſame night, Ladie *Cromwel* was
' ſtrangely tormented in her ſleep by a
' cat, (as ſhe imagined) which mother
' *Samuel* had ſent unto her, which cat of-
' fered to plucke off all the ſkin and fleſh
' from her armes and bodie.'—Was it ſo
extraordinary that ſhe ſhould have ſuch a
dream, conſidering what work ſhe had
been engaged in during the day ?—' Not
' long after the Ladie fell very ſtrangely
' ſicke, and ſo continued unto her dying
' day, which was ſome year and quarter

after

' after her being at Warboyfe. The
' manner of her fits was much like to the
' childrens, and that faying of mother
' *Samuel, (Madam, I never hurt you as yet)*
' would never out of her mind.'—The reft
of the evidence, upon which the three
Samuels were condemned for bewitching
this Lady to death, will appear in the
courfe of this hiftory.

Such multifarious wickednefs was too
much for one fpirit alone to perform; old
mother *Samuel*, therefore, and her affociates, had no lefs than nine at their command. The names of the firft fix were,
' *Pluck, Blue, Catch, White, Calico,* and
' *Hardname,* (for his name ftandeth upon
' eight letters, and every letter ftandeth
' for a word),' and that of the other three,
Smack, they being coufins: for be it known
that relationfhip exifts even amongft the
inhabitants of the nether regions. The
favourite form, under which they appeared before thofe, to whom they came to
pay their unwelcome vifits, was that of
dun chickens.

We

We shall omit many *wonders* which happened previous to that season, but we cannot forbear mentioning, that, 'towards ' Hollantide,' (probably Hallowmas, or All-Saints Day) 1592, ' the spirits grew ' very familiar with the children,' *(a most natural consequence of long acquaintance)* ' and would frequently talk with them ' halfe an hour together, and sometimes ' longer.' The general subjects of their conversation were mother *Samuel*, whom they honoured with the appellation of *Dame*, and charged with being their employer ; and the children's fits, when they should come out of them, when they should fa l into them again, and of what nature they should be.

But they did not always confine themselves to these topics, as the following specimens will evince. The oldest of these afflicted damsels, being one evening in her fit, thus addressed the visitant spirit : ' From whence come you, Master *Smack*, ' and what newes doe you bring? The ' spirite answered, that hee came from ' fighting.

' fighting.   From fighting, fayth fhe,
' with whom, I pray you?   The fpirite
' anfwered, with *Pluck*.   Where did you
' fight, I pray you, fayd fhe?   The fpirite
' anfwered, in his old Dame's back-houfe,
' and they fought with great cowlftaves,
' this laft night.   And who got the mafte-
' rie, I pray you, faid fhe?   He anfwered,
' that he broke *Pluck*'s head.   Saith fhe, I
' would that he had broke your necke alfo.
' Saith the fpirite, is that all *the thanks I*
' *fhall have for my labour?*   Why, faith
' fhe, do you look for thanks at my hands?
' I would you were all hanged up one a-
' gainft another, and your Dame and all,
' for you are all nought.   So he departed,
' and bad her farewell,' promifing to come
again on Wednefday.   Immediately afterwards came *Pluck* himfelf, hanging
down his head, and acknowledged his
unfortunate difcomfiture.

The next day fhe was vifited by Mr.
Catch, who came limping, and complained that *Smack* had broken his leg; but he
threatened to ' be even with him before
' he

' he had done. Then fayd fhe, Put forth
' your other legge, let me fee if I can
' breake that alfo; for fhee had a ftick in
' her hand: The fpirit tolde her that fhe
' could not hit him: Can I not hit you,
' fayd fhe? let me trie. Then the fpirite
' put out his legge, for fhe lifted up her
' ftick eafily, and fodaynely gave a great
' ftroake upon the ground. You have not
' hurt me, fayd the fpirit. Have I not
' hurt you, fayd fhe? but I would if I
' could, for then would I make fome of
' you come fhorte home. So fhe feemed
' divers times to ftrike at the fpirit, but
' he leaped over the fticke, as fhe fayd, as
' if it had been a *Jack an apes.* So after
' many fuch toyes ufed between them,
' the fpirit departed, and fhe came forth
' of her fit, continuing all that night, and
' the next day very ficke, and *full of payne*
' *in her legs.*' The following evening after fupper, Mafter *Blue* paid her a vifit,
with his arm in a fling, which he faid had
been broken for him by the doughty hero
Smack; yet he threatened that they would
one day fall upon him all together, and
take

take ample revenge for every injury. The
day after fhe ' fell into a fencelefs fit,' (not
recognifing any perfon prefent;) ' Anon,
' fetching a great figh, fhe faid, Who fent
' for you, Mafter *Smack?* He made an-
' fwer, that he was come according to his
' promife which he made unto her on Sun-
' daie at night. Belike, faid fhe, you
' will keep promife, but I had rather you
' would keep awaie, and come when I fend
' for you : but what news have you
' brought ? I told you that I had been a
' fighting the laft Sundaie night, but I
' have had manie battles fince. Yea, fo it
' feemeth, faith fhe, for here was both
' *Pluck*, *Catch*, and *Blew*, and they all
' came maimed unto me : But I marvel
' that you could beat them, they are very
' great, and you are but a little one. Said
' he, I am good enough for two of the
' beft of them together. But, fayd fhe, I
' can tell you news : They will all at one
' time fall upon you, and beat you. He
' faid, he cared not for that, he would beat
' two of them, and his coufin *Smacks*
' would help him to beat the other two.'
For

(For *Hardname* was alfo of the party). ' In
' the end, the fpirit fayde, You fhall have
' no more fuch fits as you have had.   No,
' fayd fhe, that is well; but you can doe
' nothing but lye.   Why, fayd hee, will
' you not beleeve me ? No, fayd fhe, fhall
' I beleeve the Divel, who is the Father
' of all lyes ?   I pray God it be true, but
' whether it be true, or not, I care not a
' rufh for you.   No, fayd he, will you
' not *thank me ?*   Thank you, fayd fhe,
' hang you and all your fellowes, for I
' will not beleeve you no farther than I
' fee you, neither do I care for any of you
' all.'—Such abfurd dialogues, of which
the narrative affords a numerous collection, fuch filly ravings of a difordered
imagination require no comment.

It ought not to be forgot, that this
Smack was peculiarly attached to this
young lady, and ftrove to gain her affec-
tions by fair promifes and kind ufage :
and it was on her account that he had
thofe gallant battles with the lefs ena-
moured fpirits, whom he beat fo unmer-

O   cifully,

cifully, becaufe they perfifted in tormenting her. The cenforious critic may perhaps fay, with a fneer, *And is it fuch an
extraordinary miracle, that love fhould occupy
the thoughts of a young lady of eighteen ?*

Soon after this familiarity commenced
between the fpirits and the children, the
former began more manifeftly to accufe
mother *Samuel*, and to fay, ere long they
'would bring her to confeffion or confufion.
The old woman refided now entirely at
Mr. *Throckmorton*'s houfe; for, contrary
to the ufual cuftom in fuch cafes, ('but
' there is no certainty in Sathan),' her prefence was a fure relief to the children.
This, however, continued only for a time,
for mother *Samuel* getting at length an
opportunity ' to feed her fpirits, and
' make a new league and compofition
' with them,' her prefence became of no
avail. Yet Mr. Throckmorton retained
her at his houfe, ' becaufe the children,
' being in their fits, could neither heare,
' fee, nor fpeake to any body elfe, and
' fome of them could take nothing, but
' that

'that which fhee either gave them or
'touched with her hands.'

And now the children were continually
teazing the old woman to confefs herfelf
guilty, affirming, that the fpirits told
them, ' they would foon enforce her to
' confefs, in defpight of herfelf,' if fhe
would not do it voluntarily: They encouraged her by promifes of forgivenefs,
to which their father and friends affented;
they entreated her with tears, faying,
that by this means fhe would certainly
relieve them, and reftore them to perfect
health ; they alfo fet before her the fevere
punifhment which fhe would inevitably
meet with both in this world and the next,
if fhe obftinately perfifted in her wickednefs. Her general anfwer was, ' That fhe
' would doe for them all the good fhe
' could, but for confeffion of this matter,
' fhe would not, for it was a thing fhe
' never knew of, nor confented unto.'

A few days before Chriftmas, one of
thefe children was attacked with a more

violent

violent fit than any of them had before experienced, yet fhe was threatened by the fpirit with one ftill more terrible. Mother *Samuel*, who was prefent, was fo affeƈted with the fight, that ' fhe many ' times prayed fhe might never fee the ' like agayne in any of them.' At the fame time the children entreated her to confefs, ' that they might be well, and ' keep a merry Chriftmas;' and their father a fo feconded their entreaties, but in vain. He then requefted Mother *Samuel* to charge the fpirit, that his daughter might efcape the fit with which fhe was threatened. ' She prefently faid, I charge thee, ' fpirit, *in the name of God*, that Miftris ' *Jane* never have this fit. The child ' fitting by, fayd, truely the thing faith, ' I thank God, that I fhall never have this ' fit that he hath foretold me of.' Again, at the father's requeft, the old woman charged the fpirit, *in the fame manner*, to leave all the children immediately, and never return to them again; fcarce had fhe uttered the words, before three of them, ' who were then in their fits, and ' had

‘ had fo continued for the fpace of three
‘ weeks, wiped their eyes, and inftantly
‘ ftood upon their legges, being as well
‘ as ever they were in their lives.’

Mother *Samuel*, as foon as fhe perceived
this, fell on her knees before Mr. *Throck-*
morton, intreating him to forgive her, and
confeffing, that fhe was the caufe of all
this trouble to his children, The next
day, fhe confirmed this confeffion publicly in the church, and in the evening was
permitted by Mr. *Throckmorton* to go home
to her hufband and daughter.

Towards the evening of the following
day, Mr. *Throckmorton* received information,
‘ that his new convert had revolted againe,
‘ and had denied all that fhe had fpoken
‘ to him ; he therefore went immediately to her, and threatened to take her
before the juftices, if fhe retracted her
former confeffion, but his threats proved
ineffectual. The next morning he fent
for her again, and fhe ftill perfifting in
the denial of her guilt, he gave the con-
ftables

ftables charge of her and her daughter, to take them before the Bifhop of Lincoln. Alarmed at this, the old woman once more offered to confefs to Mr. *Throckmorton in private*, though very averfe to doing fo *in public*. On the fame day, the 26th of December 1592, fhe was taken to *Buckden*, where, upon examination before the Bifhop of Lincoln, fhe confeffed, ‘ That a dun chicken did frequently fuck ‘ on her chin, before it came to Mr. ‘ *Throckmorton*'s houfe, and that the ill and ‘ the trouble which had come to his chil- ‘ dren, had come by means of the faid ‘ dun chicken, which fhe knew was then ‘ both gone *from them and from her.*’

On the 29th, fhe was again examined before the Bifhop, and two Juftices of the Peace, when fhe faid, ‘ That fhe never ‘ did hurt *to any, faving to the children in* ‘ *queftion;* that fhe knew the faid dun ‘ chicken was gone from the children, be- ‘ caufe the faid dun chicken, with the reft, ‘ were come *into her*, and were then in ‘ the bottom of her bellie, and made her

fo

'fo full, that fhe could fcant lace her cotc,
'and that on the way as fhe came, they
'weighed fo heavy, that the horfe fhee
'rid on did fall downe, and was not able
'to carrie her,' that fhe had received
thefe fpirits from an upright man, whofe
name fhe did not know. She then went, by
the direction of her examiners, into another room, and 'there with a loud voice, faid
'thefe words as followeth, *O thou divel, I*
'*charge thee in the name of the Father, the*
'*Son, and the Holy Ghoft, that thou tel me*
'*the name of the upright man which gave me*
'*the divels:* which thing fhe did three
'times, and then returned, faying, that
'the fpirits had tolde her his name was
'*Langland.*' In the fame manner fhe in-
quired, where he dwelt ; and the anfwer
returned was, 'That he had no dwelling.'
To the queftion, where *Langland* then
was, it was anfwered, 'that he went the
'laft voyage beyond the feas.' After fhe
had confeffed thefe, and many other things
of a fimilar nature, Mother *Samuel* was
committed, along with her daughter, to
the goal of Huntingdon.

Upon

Upon the perufal of thefe confeffions, many will be ready to embrace the opinion of thofe, whom the author of the original narrative cenfures, becaufe, 'think-'ing themfelves wife,' they did not hefi-tate to fay, ' that this Mother *Samuel* in ' queftion, was an olde fimple woman, and ' that one might make her by fayre words ' confefs what they would.' It will not efcape 'their obfervation,—that fhe never confeffed herfelf guilty, till after fhe had been affailed by reiterated folicitations, foothed by promifes, and alarmed by threats. The fpirits had alfo *predicted* her confeffion, and fhe muft have obferved how regularly *their predictions were ac-complifhed.* She faw the children relieved from their diftreffing fituation at her command. All thefe circumftances muft have had an aftonifhing effect upon a feeble and fuperftitious mind, fo that, we need not wonder, if at length they caufed her not only to fufpect herfelf, but abfolutely to conceive herfelf in league with the devil.

At

At the quarter feffions (January 9, 1593)
following the commitment of *Agnes Samuel*, and her mother, Mr. *Throckmorton*
requefted the 'High Sheriff and the Juf-
' tices to baile this maide, and to have
' her home to his houfe, to fee whether
' any fuch evidences of guiltinefs would
' appear againft her, as had before ap-
' peared in the children againft her mo-
' ther.' After fome demur his requeft
was granted, and *Agnes Samuel* accompanied him home. A few days after fhe
was brought thither, the children fell ' all
' of them a frefh into their fits, and then
' the fpirits did begin as plainly to accufe
' the daughter, as ever they did the mo-
' ther, and to tell the children, that the old
' woman hath fet over her fpirits to her
' daughter, and that fhe hath bewitched
' them all over agayne.' I fhall forbear
enumerating the various fevere fcratch-
ings which fhe underwent from each of
the children at different times, every *particular circumftance of which was invariably
foretold by the fpirits;* efpecially as fuch
ftronger proofs of her guilt were exhibit-
P   ed.

ed. For when fhe had been almoft a
month at Mr. *Throckmorton*'s, one of the
children was told by the fpirit, when in
her fit, that they fhould any of them ' be
' prefently well,' whenever *Agnes Samuel*
fhould fay, ' *I charge thee, divel, as I love*
' *thee, and am a witch, and guiltie of this*
' *matter, that thou fuffer this childe to be*
' *well at prefent.*' This was repeatedly
tried before a great variety of witneffes,
and was always attended with inftant fuccefs, though thefe words had not the leaft
effect when fpoken by any other perfon.

The fpirits alfo told the children afterwards, of other charges, by which her
guilt was made ftill more clear, fuch as,
' *I charge thee, divel, as I am a witch, and*
' *a worfer witch than my mother, and con-*
' *fenting to the death of* Ladie Crumwel :'
and, ' *As I have bewitched Mrs. Pickering*
' *of Ellington,* (an aunt of thefe children)
' *fince my mother confeffed ;*' and again, '*As*
' *I would have bewitched Miftris Joan*
' *Throckmorton to death.*'

The

The effect of thefe three charges, or charms, was repeatedly proved by different people, and even by the *Judge himfelf*, on the day before the trial of the culprits. For whenever *Agnes Samuel* called any one of thefe children out of her fit by one of thefe charges, *(particularly if any ftrangers were prefent)* fhe would almoft immediately fall into another, and after being relieved from that, into a third, till the three charges had been fucceffively proved effectual.

Laft of all, the fpirits began to accufe *John Samuel* the father, as they had before done the mother and daughter. They appealed to a charge, or charm, like the preceding ones, as a clear proof of the truth of their accufation; but from the perverfity of circumftances, and the obftinacy of the old man, this was only once proved previous to the trial of thefe three delinquents.

On the 5th of April 1593, thefe three *wicked* offenders, *John Samuel, Alice Samuel,*

P 2   and

and *Agnes* their daughter, were arraigned
before Mr. Juſtice *Fenner*, ‘ for bewitch-
‘ ing of the Ladie *Cromwal* to death ; and
‘ for bewitching of Miſtreſs *Joane Throck-*
‘ *morton*, Miſtris *Jane Throckmorton*, and
‘ others;’ when ‘Maſter*Dorrington*, Doᵗor
‘ of Divinitie, and parſon of the town of
‘ Warboyſe, *Thomas Nut*, Maſter of Arte,
‘ and viçar of Ellington,’ the father of
theſe afflicted children, and others of their
relations, appeared as evidence againſt
them. By theſe the before related
‘ proofs, preſumptions, circumſtances, and
‘ reaſons,’ with many others of the ſame
ſpecies, ‘ were at large delivered, untill
‘ both the Judge, Juſtices, and Jury ſaid
‘ openly, that the cauſe was moſt ap-
‘ parant; their conſciences were well ſa-
‘ tisfied, that the ſayd witches were guil-
‘ tie, and had deſerved death.’ As to
John Samuel, *occular* proof of his guilt
was exhibited in court. For amongſt the
reſt ‘ Miſtrifs *Jane Throckmorton* was
‘ brought into court,’ and there, in her
fit, unable to ſpeak, or ſee any one,
though ‘ her eyes were open,’ ſhe was ſet
before

before the Judge, who was told that there
was a charm, which ' if old *Samuel* would
' fpeake, the fayd *Jane* fhould be well.'
In confequence of which information, he
was requefted by the Judge to repeat the
charm, but this he pofitively refufed to
do, till threatened, that if he perfifted in
his obftinate refufal, ' the court would
' hold him guiltie of the crimes whereof
' he was accufed.' Intimidated by this
threat, he at length complied, ' and faid,
' in the hearing of all that were prefent,
' *As I am a witch, and did confent to the*
' *death of Ladie* CROMWELL, *fo I charge*
' *thee divell, to fuffer Miftrifs* JANE *to*
' *come out of her fit at this prefent.*' Which
words being no fooner fpoken by ' the old
' witch, but the faid Miftris *Jane*, as her
' accuftomed order was, wiped her eyes,
' and came out of her fit.' The Judge
immediately obferved, ' *You fee all fhee is*
' *now well, but not with the muficke of Da-*
' *vid's harpe.*'—We muft not forget, that
the fpirit had *previoufly told this* Miftris
Jane, when fhe was firft feized, on the
16th of March, ' that fhe fhould never
' come

' come out of her fit, until old father *Sa-*
' *muel* had pronounced thefe wordes.'

When the Judge, previous to paffing of
fentence, afked Mother *Samuel* the ufual
queftion, What have you to fay for your-
felf, why fentence of death fhould not be
pronounced upon you? She anfwered,
that *fhe was with child.* Such a plea
from a woman of near eighty years of
age, excited the laughter of all prefent,
and the old woman ' laughed herfelf more
' than any other.'—Could a ftronger proof
of her dotage or infanity be poffibly exhibited?

At the place of execution, old *Alice*
Samuel again confeffed her guilt, and that
her hufband was her affociate in thefe
wicked proceedings, though he refolutely
denied it to the laft. Her daughter fhe
ftrenuoufly exculpated, who as warmly
afferted her own innocence; ' but being
' willed to fay the Lord's prayer and the
' creed, when, as fhe ftood upon the lad-
' der

(129)

' der readie to be executed, she sayd the
' Lord's prayer, until she came to say, *but*
' *deliver us from evil*, the which she could
' by no means pronounce ; and in the
' creed she missed very much, and could
' not say, *that she believed in the Catholic
' church.*'—A circumstance amply sufficient
to convince every one that she could not
possibly be *innocent*.

To this narrative, so fertile in ' proofs,
' presumptions, circumstances, and rea-
sons,' we shall add no further observa-
tion, though it furnishes such an ample
field for comment, fully persuaded, that
its *consistency, clearness*, and *probability* are
sufficient to remove every doubt and hesi-
tation from the mind of the reader.

F I N I S.

www.ingramcontent.com/pod-product-compliance
Ingram Content Group UK Ltd.
Pitfield, Milton Keynes, MK11 3LW, UK
UKHW042151280225
455719UK00001B/272